PHILIP LARKIN

HIS LIFE'S WORK

PHILIP LARKIN
HIS LIFE'S WORK

Janice Rossen

University of Iowa Press, Iowa City

For John Augustine,
a stalwart friend

'You can be any sort of man and be a poet.'

Edmund Crispin, *The Moving Toyshop*

Contents

Preface

In the course of an outwardly sedate and decorous life, Philip Larkin
wore a number of different hats: distinguished poet, Oxford
University. graduate, 'Unofficial Laureate', Librarian of the
University of Hull, Honorary Doctor of Letters, Companion of
Literature, and jazz critic, to name only a few. Yet if his notion
holds true that the best poetry reflects one's own experience, he also
possessed the hidden shades of a man who knew and who shrewdly
observed Mr Bleaney, Dockery, Arnold, and Warlock-Williams in
himself and in others – and moreover, who could write about them
in funny and scathingly grim verse. Though not exactly an *enfant
terrible* of the order of Kingsley Amis, Larkin possessed a threatening
presence in this vein as well; he did not suffer fools at all gladly and
for this reason was a man one feared to displease. At the same time,
his book reviews and jazz criticism show as enthusiastic an
appreciation of what he liked as they did a severe denunciation of
what he disliked. His interests were diverse yet well considered, and
above all firmly entrenched; he complained ceaselessly about the
'aberration of Modernism', and he championed the cause of the
Royal Society for the Prevention of Cruelty to Animals. He showed
enormous tact, courtesy and kindness as well.

His poetry has a peculiar power and stringency, sparked with
occasional bitterness. His satires, complaints, dirges, meditations and
lyrics show an impressive range of poetic voices – and they delight
because of their technical skill (he is a formal poet) and their
inventive playfulness and wit. His work is both clear and elusive,
precise and complex. This book looks closely at the influence of
Yeats and Hardy on the development of Larkin's style, and at his
covert romanticism as it relates to nature in general and to England
in particular. It also discusses his views of male sexual desire, his
artistic opinions as vigorously expressed in his prose writings as well

as his poetry, and the dialectic created throughout his work between wit and pessimism, toads and melancholy, the daily grind of work and 'another step down Cemetery Road'.

Janice Rossen
University of Texas, Austin

Acknowledgements

Thanks are due to the British Library, London, the Bodleian Library, Oxford, the Brynmor Jones Library, Hull, the University of Victoria Library, Victoria, and the Huntington Library, San Marino for the invaluable research assistance I received from members of their staffs. I am indebted to several fine librarians for their advice and help. I am particularly grateful to Brian Dyson, Archivist at the Brynmor Jones Library, who allowed me to see the collection which formed the Larkin exhibition assembled by himself, Maeve M. Brennan, and Geoff Weston, and which was mounted at the University of Hull in 1986. Anthony Thwaite generously allowed me to look through some of Larkin's un-published material. I am also grateful to Macmillan for allowing me to reprint an altered version of the essay 'Larkin Abroad' which appeared in Dale Salwak's edited collection, *Philip Larkin: The man and his work*. I would especially like to thank Larkin's literary executors, Anthony Thwaite, Monica Jones, Andrew Motion and Terence Wheldon, for allowing me to quote from unpublished letters and poems, and for assisting me in many other ways as well.

Copyright material: reprinted by permission of Faber and Faber Ltd from *Collected Poems*, *The North Ship*, *The Whitsun Weddings*, *High Windows*, *All What Jazz*, *Required Writing*, *A Girl in Winter* and *Jill* by Philip Larkin. From *Jill* by Philip Larkin, Copyright © 1976 Philip Larkin. Published by The Overlook Press, Lewis Hollow Road, Woodstock, New York. Excerpts from *High Windows* by Philip Larkin. Copyright © 1974 by Philip Larkin. Reprinted by permission of Farrar, Straus and Giroux, Inc. Excerpts from *Required Writing* by Philip Larkin. Copyright © 1982, 1983 by Philip Larkin. Reprinted by permission of Farrar, Straus and Giroux, Inc. 'Toads', 'Triple Time', 'At Grass', 'Next, Please', 'Wants', 'Poetry of Departures', 'Wedding Wind', 'Absences', 'Coming', 'Church Going', 'Places,

Loved Ones', 'Spring', 'I Remember, I Remember', and 'Reasons for Attendance' by Philip Larkin are reprinted from *The Less Deceived* by permission of The Marvell Press, England.

Ackowledgement is also made to Victor Gollancz to quote from Kingsley Amis' *Lucky Jim*; and Chatto & Windus to quote from Andrew Motion's *Natural Causes*. Special thanks to the estate of Philip Larkin for permission to quote extracts from unpublished sources of material, as well as to Alistair Wilson and the BBC for permission to quote from his radio programme 'The bicycle-clipped misanthropist'. I am also grateful to individual holders of letters for permission to quote extracts, including Douglas Dunn, Andrew Motion, Betty Mackereth, Maeve M. Brennan, Mary Judd, Professor Garnet Rees and the estate of Sir John Betjeman. Many thanks to Brian Dyson and the Brynmor Jones Library for allowing me to consult and to quote from Larkin's letters to James Sutton. I would also like to thank Kenneth Hibbert for permission to quote from Larkin's unpublished poem 'Booze', written in a 'Christmas card' to him. Every effort has been made to trace all copyright holders, but if any have been inadvertently overlooked, the publishers will be pleased to make the necessary arrangements at the first opportunity.

Several people were extremely gracious in sharing with me their insights into Larkin's life and poetry, and I am grateful to them for many interesting conversations and enjoyable meals. My thanks go to Charles Monteith, Douglas Dunn, Hilary Pym Walton, J. R. Watson of the University of Durham, Jean Hartley, Virginia Peace of the University of Hull, Brenda Moon of the University of Edinburgh, Professor Garnet and Dilys Rees of the University of Hull, John and Gaynor Woodhouse of Pembroke College, Oxford, B. C. Bloomfield of the British Library, Anthony Thwaite of André Deutsch, Andrew Motion of Chatto & Windus, Brian Dyson and Maeve M. Brennan of the Brynmor Jones Library, Professor Douglas Gray of the University of Oxford, Barbara Everett of Somerville College, Oxford, and Kingsley Amis.

On this side of the Atlantic, conversations with a number of people helped to clarify my thinking, and I would like especially to thank Terry and Laura Mathis, Anne Wyatt-Brown, Metche Alexander, David Braun, and Thomas Caramagno. For the writing of the book, I am very much indebted to John Augustine and Maeve M. Brennan, who read drafts of the manuscript in various stages, and also to Jean Wyatt and Dale Salwak, who gave excellent advice on several points. Thanks also go to Andrew McClure for his research assistance. Jerome Meckier, Peter Firchow and Norman

Fruman contributed to the shaping of this study both directly and indirectly, and I am grateful for their encouragement. William Rossen several times helpfully suggested a reading of *Lucky Jim* as an antidote to melancholy, and remained unfailing in his kindness and interest during the years which saw the writing of this book and (on his part) of several scientific research papers. I also owe a great debt to the late Henri Coulette, with whom I spent many hours discussing poetry, academic politics, scholarly pursuits, and the misery and absurdity of life in general. I shall miss him immensely.

Abbreviations

Page numbers are noted in brackets within the text, using the following abbreviations:

> J   *Jill* (1946)
> GW *A Girl in Winter* (1947)
> AWJ *All What Jazz* (1970)
> RW *Required Writing* (1983)
> CP   *Collected Poems* (1988)

The *Collected Poems* (London: Faber & Faber, 1988) includes *The North Ship* (1945), *The Whitsun Weddings* (1964), and *High Windows* (1974), the rights to which are owned by Faber & Faber (as are those for the prose volumes) and *The Less Deceived* (1955), the rights to which are owned by the Marvell Press. The editions to which page numbers refer are: *Jill* (London: The Fortune Press, 1946), *A Girl in Winter* (London: Faber & Faber, 1947), *All What Jazz* (London: Faber & Faber, revised edition, rpt 1985), and *Required Writing* (London: Faber & Faber, 1983).

Introduction

'Whatever a poet is supposed to look like, it's not me', Larkin once declared in an interview, and this remark hints at his usual *modus operandi*; he is constantly sending himself up.[1] He discounts what little he does say in public as mere role-playing; 'I don't want to go around pretending to be me', he once remarked, by way of explaining his reluctance to give public poetry readings and academic lectures (*RW*, 51). Yet although he made much of his refusal to become a public figure – even to declining the Laureateship – this seems in part a pose taken to intrigue the public to whom he professed indifference. His self-deprecation would not delight his admirers or irritate his detractors so hugely if it were not in part a vast private joke, underlined by a craftsmanlike and admirable body of work – and a formidable literary reputation. In consequence, his elusiveness has become almost as notable as his fame.

Larkin drew a strict division between his public and private lives. He succeeded in isolating himself from the London literary community by moving to Hull in 1955 to take the post of Librarian at the University of Hull, where he remained until his death in December of 1985. Several obituaries referred to him as 'The Hermit of Hull', an epithet which Larkin had given grounds for by stating that he felt a need to be 'on the periphery' of the literary world – indeed, on the periphery of England itself (*RW*, 55). Even within the realm in which he lived, he claimed ignorance of what went on around him. He wrote to Barbara Pym that he could not advise her on a novel about provincial university life because he knew nothing of it: 'As a librarian, I'm remote from teaching, examining, and research; as a bachelor I'm remote from the Wives' Club or the Ups and Downs of Entertaining; as an introvert I hardly notice anything anyway.'[2] He delighted in playing the role of recluse. 'I was asked to [the Byron unveiling]', he wrote to Pym on one occasion, 'but since so much of my reputation seems to depend on never being seen anywhere (as meretricious, really, as the reverse, only much pleasanter) I didn't go.'[3]

Even so, Larkin had a convivial side as well, and was valued by his friends as a lively and witty conversationalist. He once quipped that he did not buy a dining table for his flat, since if he did he would have to have people to dinner; but in fact he often took friends out to eat, and habitually accepted invitations to other people's homes, being apt himself to turn up unexpectedly on a friend's doorstep of a Sunday afternoon.[4] Rather than casting him as a recluse, it might be more accurate to think of him as having a kind of love/hate relationship with social events – or with people in general. One of the many stories about him which shows him figuratively defending his own territory records the following incident: 'Once, waiting at a bus-stop in torrential rain, Neville [Smith] edged closer and closer to Larkin, who had an umbrella. Finally the poet spoke: "Don't think you're going to share my umbrella because you're not." '[5] Larkin could also be severe on the subject of planned arrangements: 'I'm not kidding when I say I don't like meeting literary chaps', he wrote to Douglas Dunn, although he did know several other writers and often attended parties where they were present. What he most desired was to be able to decline company when he chose to do so. In another letter to Dunn, Larkin identifies himself with the speaker in '*Vers de Société*', mentioning almost with satisfaction that a particular physical pain 'proves a useful excuse to dodge evenings w. W-Wm's'.[6]

Larkin's writing has earned him a high reputation. His first volume of poetry, *The North Ship* (1945), was followed by two novels, *Jill* (1946) and *A Girl in Winter* (1947), and by three more volumes of poetry: *The Less Deceived* (1955), *The Whitsun Weddings* (1964) and *High Windows* (1974). Collections of his jazz criticism, book reviews, and various prose pieces appeared under the titles *All What Jazz* (1970) and *Required Writing* (1983). One difficulty in assessing his work arises from the fact that much of his contribution to the development of twentieth-century poetry was to write more traditional, formal verse; it is tempting to see this as an artistic regression rather than an advance. Although Larkin influenced several younger writers, admiration for his work was by no means universal. In his study of contemporary British poets, Weatherhead points out that 'Poets of the generation following the Movement writers (a generation in these swift times being about five years) reproved their predecessors for the old style ... and [for] having avoided the horrors that were rife in man's broadest experiences of the world.[7] If, as John Wain has suggested, Larkin 'rescued' poetry from the aberration of Modernism, it does not seem to have stayed rescued.

In one sense, Larkin's detractors have done him a favour by not allowing his literary reputation to become over-valued. The shape of his writing career has also contributed to his unusual relationship with the literary community – though he was honoured for his work, success came too late to allow him to assimilate easily into the contemporary literary world, especially given his mildly suspicious and reclusive character. By the time of his full-scale lionisation, Larkin had become withdrawn and disappointed about what he considered to be his relative lack of success. After a false start in the 1940s (three books which received almost no notice), his work did, of course, become widely appreciated. When his second volume, *The Less Deceived*, appeared in 1955 it received attention, then popular and critical acclaim, and finally renown. Still, it was a problematic kind of success because of what it did not confer: he was acknowledged as a poet, but not as a novelist. Most immediately, the volume brought him recognition as part of the Movement, a group of 1950s poets. Larkin contributed to Robert Conquest's anthology *New Lines*, and to D. J. Enright's *Poets of the 1950s*, both of which became standard texts which illustrated the group's proclivities.[8] As Larkin himself pointed out, though, the group was not particularly close-knit, nor did its members have much in common; and he did not especially care about them anyway.

By contrast, Larkin was never seen as one of the so-called Angry Young Men, novelists and playwrights such as Wain, Braine, Osborne, Sillitoe and Amis, who all became quite celebrated early in their writing careers. Though Larkin shared many of their sensibilities and was a friend of some of these writers, he did not write satirical novels, and thus could not be included in this group; nor could he reap the advantages they enjoyed. His two novels from the 1940s were in a tradition of psychological realism – and were not of a kind to make a splash, unlike many of the 'Angry' novels, which received great amounts of publicity and a number of which were made into successful films. Although one cannot compare Larkin's experience directly to that of the 'Angries', it casts some new light on the subject of his artistic development to see it in this context; at least initially, his writing did not bring him the recognition he desired and which they received. In a purely personal sense, and unrelated to the question of which group he belonged to, his emergence as a poet rather than a novelist disappointed him because his driving ambition as a young man had been to achieve fame as a novelist – and because the financial rewards for writing poetry were not as great as he had imagined those for writing novels might be. He was never able to devote himself to writing full time, and this added to the sense of frustration which he felt about his writing, when he occasionally wondered if it might have been different in quantity or quality had he been able to devote all his energies to it.

In effect, Larkin suffered something of a check in his literary career as a result of not being admired and lionised early on as many of his contemporaries were. This may seem insignificant in the light of later, well-deserved praise – the unofficial title of 'the Other Laureate', the Queen's Gold Medal for Poetry, honorary doctorates, a multitude of invitations to teach and lecture – all of which delighted him immensely. Yet it is possible that the recognition came too late to affect substantially the way in which he saw his writing career, or that it came in a tiresome form. The habitual sense of wry comedy with which Larkin addressed everything was applied to the subject of his literary reputation, even as it continued to increase. He wrote to Douglas Dunn about one occasion on which he had received an award: 'I am glad the Palace is over: I found it rather an ordeal, not being one of nature's courtiers. It was terribly tedious, too – lots of standing and sitting about. However, it was all extremely well meant, and I got through it without being taken to the Tower.'[9] His keen relish in self-mockery hints at private, wounded vanity, in addition to providing a way to devalue it for himself. He took great delight, for instance, in telling friends that the Queen's Gold Medal for Poetry arrived by post one morning while he was shaving.[10] His public remark on the subject of the honour was elaborately self-deprecating: 'Taking this Queen's Medal. I'm 42, but [W. H. Auden] got it for "Look Stranger" when he was 30.'[11] An honour could also be seen to herald advancing old age and to reflect on a career which had already run its full course; receiving an honorary doctorate from Oxford finds him possessed of 'a sort of *nunc dimittis* feeling', as he jokes about it.[12] Yet one suspects that the wealth of honours gratified him enormously, and offered a much-desired validation of his work; the Gold Medal found him writing to fellow craftsman Sir John Betjeman that he 'need never write another line now'.[13]

Still, the tedium of public occasions (additionally made difficult by his increasing deafness in later years) was keenly felt, as he wrote to Pym about one such ordeal, when he received the Companion of Literature award: 'Like all RSL occasions I've attended it seemed for them rather than us – no one introduced me to the Duke, or really paid much attention at all, except for bores who wrote children's books, etc.'[14] This is rather shabby treatment, at least as he describes it, and lionisation like this is not greatly to be valued. One can sympathise with him; as Andrew Motion aptly states, Larkin's many honours were 'accompanied by publicity from which he ... assiduously defended himself'.[15] His relationship with the outside world is a complex one in that he shows himself acutely sensitive to what others might think, and he seems unable to protect himself from slights (whether real or imagined). As he wrote to his friend James Sutton while still in his twenties, 'great men have great energy', and it is largely unaffected by outside checks: 'they are those lucky beings in whom a horny sheath of egoism protects their energy, not allowing it to be dissipated or turned against itself.'[16] He would have wished to possess such sturdy indifference himself.

At the same time, his aloofness from publicity allowed Larkin to keep his anger alive and scintillating; he courted a private contempt for the literary world and the judgements of others. He commented on artistic matters at length – the jazz criticism, book reviews and editing of the *Oxford Book of Twentieth Century Verse* are cases in point – but by staying in Hull as he did for so many years, and by not living in London, he remained freer to pronounce on his likes and dislikes. And, although he made frequent trips to London and Oxford, he could always retreat to the seclusion of Hull, where few would come to find him.

Despite this highly ambivalent relationship with the outside world, his reputation has continued to increase. Larkin is fast becoming 'a name to conjure with', as he himself once phrased it.[17] The way in which he perceived his own achievement seems important when one considers his life's work, and much of this study is based on a biographical approach to his poetry. It makes use where possible of Larkin's letters, of his working notebook donated to the British Museum, and of conversations with several people who knew Larkin, both fellow poets and friends. Starting from the point of his stylistic development between *The North Ship* and *The Less Deceived*, the book considers the symbolist side of his work in his attitude to nature, and then to England. It turns next to his discussion of the problems of the middle-aged bachelor and of 'difficulties with girls', going on to address the way in which his opinions are expressed in strong language in his prose writings, book reviews, jazz criticism and poetry. The final chapter considers the correlation between his extreme pessimism and the witty complaints which he makes against the frustrations he encounters in everyday life.

1

Becoming a Poet

The North Ship to *The Less Deceived*, 1945–55

Barbara Everett has suggested that Larkin's 'three volumes of major verse are the odd, reticent triumph of a self-undercutting artist whose skills make him a "secret poet" as some men are secret agents or secret drinkers.'[1] There is an air of deliberately suggested modesty about Larkin's poetry that springs from his self-adopted role as 'librarian poet', writing a few lines of verse in the evening after doing the washing up. In later interviews, Larkin agrees politely that he would possibly have liked to have made a full-time career of it, but that the times were not propitious: 'I could never have made a living from writing. If I'd tried in the Forties and Fifties I'd have been a heap of whitened bones long ago' (*RW*, 51). Accordingly, Larkin's public has almost come to expect this typical self-deprecation, though as Everett writes elsewhere, the accessibility of his work to his readers does not make him simply 'one of us'; there is clearly something that sets Larkin apart in his ability to write poetry dazzlingly well.[2] Curiously, however, one of Larkin's driving ambitions at one time was to be a full-time novelist modelled on a glamorous, expatriate, Robert Graves kind of figure, living and writing as he described it 'on the Côte d'Azur, uninterrupted except for the correction of proofs' (*RW*, 49). Since he became a university librarian in the north of England instead, this fantasy subsequently became a joke which Larkin made in order to underline the ordinariness of his career. As it was, he often referred to a small event, such as moving from his rented flat into a house, as being a decisive factor in adversely affecting his creative process. Speaking of the eighteen years of his tenancy in the flat at Pearson Park, Larkin once joked to Charles Monteith: 'You must never forget, Charles, that that was my Great Period.'[3]

Yet behind the elaborate mockery of himself as a writer lies an earnestness and single-minded concentration which is evident from early on during Larkin's Oxford years, when he wrote to schoolfriend (and fellow aspiring artist) James Sutton, 'I say a great deal that I am "great" or that you are "great" but I really believe it; and if I don't become some kind of a good writer I shall turn from life in disgust as being totally false, and feelings as being quite untrustworthy.'[4] This conviction was off-set, of course, by moments of great anxiety, if only because to succeed as a writer *meant* so much to him; when he reread a draft version of his first novel, *Jill*, he confided to Sutton: 'God, writing is fucking hard. I doubt – I doubt.'[5] And always, he resorted to the intermittent burst of humorous self-parody to lighten the burden: 'Horrible feeling I can't write away from Coventry. Profound, sickening, and unescapable [sic] conclusion. I am not, nor ever shall be, a writer. God! fetch me that gin, boy. Upward.'[6] Secret drinking possesses some mysterious link with secret poetry writing, in that it at least causes one to forget one's failure in creativity (in Larkin's case, not writing a novel). And the necessity of secrecy in both endeavours springs from fearing failure in writing – an anxiety which always runs close to the surface of Larkin's comments about his own work.

There is, in short, an inherent paradox in our view of Larkin's creative process, especially in light of his later, self-created reputation as a 'minor poet' – he appears, at times, almost a comical bungler. He is perceived by many critics as drawing his strength from a consummate ordinariness, in which vein he writes to and for the common man – and about subjects or experiences for which he tries, as he himself says, 'to find a combination of words that will preserve it by setting it off in other people' (*RW*, 58). His precision and clarity have often been praised. But his work has also been characterised as excessively 'genteel' or narrow or conservative.[7] In a peculiar combination of attributes, Larkin seems to write for the common man but also *as* a common man ('a provincial gentleman intellectual,' as J. R. Watson characterises this view, in order to deplore it), and to write somehow too little and too far away to be taken seriously as a major force.[8] Criticism of his poetry has become, in broad outlines, a struggle between those who accuse Larkin of narrowness and those who defend him as an important poet.[9]

A crucial subject for discussion in this debate about Larkin's literary achievement is his marked development in poetic style between his first and second volumes, *The North Ship* (1945) and *The Less Deceived* (1955). Larkin's creative process is, in general, so little understood and the source of his poetic genius so obscured (since usually labelled as 'ordinary'), that it has become difficult to see clearly the development of his career. And this is especially true in what is perhaps its most important transition, the decade of 1945–55. There is no doubt that the change during the period between these first two poetry collections was a significant one, as *The Less Deceived* first forged the style which was to become so celebrated in the larger movement away from Modernism (the effect of 'those two Americans', as Wain typifies it) and toward a spare Anglican style.[10]

Larkin himself ascribed the change to a shift in poetic influence which occurred during this time, namely a 'conversion' from Yeats to Hardy. In the introduction to a reissue of *The North Ship* twenty years later, he described an 'infatuation' with Yeats after his initial discovery of Yeats' writing, made through the poet Vernon Watkins. This was followed by a period of literary apprenticeship: 'As a result I spent the next three years trying to write like Yeats' (*RW*, 29). Larkin described his subsequent conversion to Thomas Hardy as having been due to the almost accidental choice of 'the little blue *Chosen Poems of Thomas Hardy*' as habitual morning reading when 'the sun woke [him] inconveniently early' in new digs which faced east (*RW*, 29). This explanation seems plausible, especially because of its concrete detail. Still, several critics have rightly suspected the sweeping nature of such a claim. Grevel Lindop enquires: 'Was ever a professional librarian and dedicated poet so mercilessly pushed about by a couple of stray books? Really, the story won't stand a great deal of scrutiny.'[11] John Press comments also on the enigmatic nature of the transformaton: 'It is difficult to believe that a mere switch of literary allegiance could have brought about so remarkable a change.'[12] Indeed, Larkin's transformation resulted less from the effect of outside literary influence than it did from his doubts about his own literary ability.

Within this decade of transformation, one theme seems to dominate Larkin's thoughts: that of failure, and of early promise having been 'Quickly consumed,' as the poem 'On Being Twenty-Six' phrases it (*CP*, 24). In terms of his publishing record, he certainly began well, bringing out *The North Ship* in 1945, *Jill* in 1946, and *A Girl in Winter* in 1947. Yet the period between 1948 and 1955, when *The Less Deceived* appeared, seemed anything but auspicious, beginning as it did with the rejection of Larkin's second volume of poetry, *In the Grip of Light*, which he sent out for publication in 1948. The volume was considered and subsequently refused by six publishers.[13] In the end, the collection was never published entire, though individual poems from the volume appeared in *XX Poems*, a selection which Larkin published privately in 1951, and finally in *The Less Deceived* in 1955. Both facts – the rejection by publishers of *In the Grip of Light* and the excellence of *The Less Deceived* – have surprising implications, when the connection between them is examined in light of what the latter volume represents in larger terms. It seems quite possible, in fact, that the immense sense of rejection and disappointment which Larkin must have felt at this juncture, upon the rejection of his second volume of poetry, had profound implications for his writing; he continued to write poetry after the book was rejected – but to write poetry about rejection and failure.

Several other important events occurred during this period as well, which combined to influence Larkin and his writing during his mid-twenties and early thirties: the death of his father in 1948 and Larkin's subsequent living with and caring for his widowed mother until his move to Belfast; his becoming engaged, then unengaged, then increasingly uncertain about whether to marry at all; his moves to a succession of library posts and his taking official qualifying exams to become a librarian; and his continuing inability to write the third novel which he so desperately wanted to write following *Jill* and *A Girl in Winter*. Larkin was also (as he remained in later years) keenly aware of the passing of time in relation to his own creative ambitions; a poem such as 'On Being Twenty-six' finds him dreading this stage in his life:

> I feared these present years,
>   The middle twenties,
> When deftness disappears,
> And each event is
> Freighted with a source-encrusting doubt,
>   And turned to drought.
>
> (*CP*, 24)

In retrospect, he feels that both his ability and his ambition have been 'Quickly consumed in me, / As I foresaw', thus suggesting that he expected or feared a falling-off in his writing powers (*CP*, 24). Similarly, the poem 'At thirty-one, when some are rich' restates the theme of unfulfilled promise a few short years later. 'At thirty-one, when some are rich / And others dead, / I, being neither, have a job instead' he writes caustically (*CP*, 69).

An important aspect of this decade for Larkin, then, was the harrowing sense of time running out while the prize of literary recognition seemed to recede further and further. Alan Brownjohn refers to these years as a 'long and disheartening period of transition,' concluding that 'In the early 1950s [Larkin] might have felt that he had written himself into failure.'[14] And yet it is possible that through the process of internalising and dealing with his pain and frustration, just the opposite occurred: Larkin wrote himself out of failure and into an immediate, vivid poetic style, by tackling this problem in his writing. By 1955 he had definitely found his own distinctive poetic voice; and much of this change can be traced to this period of thwarted ambition, as his working notebook from the period 1944–50 indicates, in conjunction with his letters from the time to his schoolfriend James Sutton, which chart the history of his literary ambitions while Larkin was up at Oxford and through his twenties.

From at least his late teen years, Larkin marked himself out for a serious writer. He began writing poetry at the age of about fifteen, and was writing both poems and novels while up at Oxford. Even early on, he felt that the latter were a superior form. He wrote to Sutton in 1940: 'Novels are better. A novel should be a diffused poem,' adding that a 'Novel's ten thousand times harder than poems. Probably better, too.'[15] This passage in the letters shows his early thinking on the subject, and it also marks the first mention of the novel which would eventually become *Jill*. But he also formulated a finer distinction than that between novels as 'better' or 'harder' than poetry – namely, poetry is seen here in romantic terms, and has entirely to do with a received vision. Larkin declared that he is 'against this poetry-as-a-craft business,' and described the creative process as being one which occurs 'because the poet gets a sudden vision – lasting one second or less – and he attempts to express the whole of which the vision is part.'[16] This implies that there is still some creative work for the poet to undertake, as he is required to see a partial vision and express a whole one, but it seems primarily a matter of inspiration rather than of artifice. Further, in this scheme the means of writing is done 'quite intuitively and esoterically', and thus without regard for the reader: 'That is why a poet never thinks of his reader. Why should he? The reader doesn't come into the poem at all.'[17] This is an important point, because it seems to contribute to his ability to write poetry later on, while in his late twenties, when he was struggling to continue creating after the disappointment of not being able to write a novel; in other words, Larkin's success in writing (at least for the first decade or so in his literary career) stems in part from his ability to ignore the reader

altogether, as evidenced in poems such as 'Fiction and the Reading
Public', which was designed to mock and distance his audience. And
he made that connection in his first few years as a writer, namely
that of the poet *not* having to please the reader, a principle which
seems to have helped him so much that he continued to adopt it
throughout his career.

These strategies address the problem of fearing to take
responsibility for one's work, lest it turn out to be lacking in quality
or verve and thus reflect badly on one's identity as an artist. In a
much later letter to Sutton, written in 1949, Larkin goes still further
in this view, ascribing nearly everything to fate: 'Life is chiefly an
affair of "life-force": we are varyingly charged with it and that
represents our energy and nothing we do or so [sic] will alter our
voltage or wattage.'[18] This embracing of determinism forms part of
the general pattern which he established in order to be able to write.
In order to forestall excessive criticism, which might have
hampered him from creating, he employed various techniques to
distance the reader, to place responsibility for writing on to a 'life-
force' or onto the poet's received 'vision', and therefore to lighten
the pressure of expectation that he would produce excellent work.

As suggested earlier, this was the more necessary as he had
determined with a fierceness amounting to desperation that he must
become a writer or life itself would be false. As for the poetry
which Larkin wrote while at Oxford, its creation generally seems to
have constituted a long period of apprenticeship under various poets
(Auden, Isherwood, Lawrence, Yeats and others) and of trying to
determine his own value as a poet in relation to them. He was
self-conscious about both his possibly overpraising his work and the
fact that it mattered so much to him. At one point, he copied out
some early poems for Sutton, commenting 'I think this is balling
bloody cunting fucking good. Much nearer Lawrence than Auden,
anyway. And written when I was *sixteen*!! God'[19] Doubts about
necessarily remaining a 'minor artist' or even suffering under an
inability to 'be anything at all' continued to plague him, and he
existed in a tension between feeling alternately a genius or a fool.[20]
One concise summary of this occurs when he astutely separated two
voices within himself, 'one of which says I am a damn' fine man,
remarkably sensitive, peculiarly gifted and certain to be a good
writer.' Its counterpart, however, declared that 'I am a nervous sod,
who in order to compensate a whacking great inferiority complex
has built up a dream-world about myself, totally devoid of reality or
substance.'[21] In effect, his violent mood swings made him

determined to distrust himself, and lead eventually to a resolve to be, in his now famous phrase, 'less deceived' about his views of himself and the world.

In fact, in addition to reading Yeats and Auden while at Oxford, Larkin also read D. H. Lawrence and Freud, and it is perhaps from the psychology which he was covertly studying that the phrase 'the less deceived' derived. The letter to Sutton in 1949 which mentions the inevitable power of the 'life-force' finds Larkin using the curious phrase, 'I search myself for illusions like a monkey looking for fleas,' and concluding 'that any ideas about life are almost certain to be wrong.'[22] This willed distrust of his own ability to see life clearly and rationally could have seemed a grim necessity to him, especially after suffering disappointments over his work and the way it was received; but it could also have tended to make the inspirational and creative springs of poetry or fiction writing dry up. In adopting this scheme, he necessarily became highly critical of his own work, of himself, and of the characters he created in novels. The attempt to become 'less deceived' probably constituted a mixed blessing, in that it made him less able to tolerate the sense of flux and uncertainty which was necessary for the early stages of creating. As he wrote to Sutton in 1942, 'Having read Lawrence, [the best novelist ever, in Larkin's view] I know what shit is, and won't write it: on the other hand, I can't write anything else. Hence a state of deadlock.'[23] This seems a clear recipe for writer's block, and shows, I think, how the strategy sabotaged itself to some extent. In addition, although he tried to think in a Freudian framework and tended to regard himself as neurotic, he seems to have been unable to make the connection between his inability to write novels and the fact that the effect of neurotic guilt might have prevented him from doing just that. If part of his psyche was intent on not allowing him pleasure, and he defined novel writing as his most desired object, this would pose difficulties in achieving that aim. Also – though not to push this idea too far – it seems possible that his huge admiration for Lawrence might have made novel writing extremely difficult simply because Larkin could not figuratively replace, match or overthrow him as a patriarchal figure. Writing poetry rather than novels thus allowed him (possibly unconsciously) to write around the overwhelming figure of Lawrence as novelist, yet still to follow in the footsteps of his chosen mentor, who also wrote in both genres.

Larkin seems to have relied largely on a combination of inspiration and sheer hard work to write novels. The plan which he devised for *Jill* and *A Girl in Winter* carried on the romantic view of writing which he formulated in his first year at Oxford. *Jill* was initially to be 'about somebody who "needs love"' as he wrote to Sutton on first mentioning the idea.[24] He envisioned the second novel, originally titled *The Kingdom of Winter*, as a kind of sequel to *Jill*: it 'has for theme the relinquishing of live response to life. The central character, Katherine, picks up where John left off and carries the story out into the frozen wastes.'[25] These themes in many ways echo those in *The North Ship*, which often deal with coldness, loneliness, and loss of love – and they suggest, to some extent, his anxious state of mind at the time.

The publication of *The North Ship*, *Jill*, and *A Girl in Winter* all in the space of three years, must have been an exhilarating experience, and probably confirmed his vision of himself as someone who could write. Yet Larkin's agonised self-consciousness about these books seems immense, and it continued long after they appeared in print. He virtually apologised to Sutton, when he wrote to his friend asking permission to dedicate the novel *Jill* to him, adding: 'In its defence I would say I spent a year on it, working really hard, and some bits are amusing. You may not like it as a whole, but it is the first fruits of a properly-clarified effort, and it is as good as I could do at 21–22.'[26] Once accepted, the book took a long time to appear and he found waiting almost unbearable; 'God bugger me blue, where *is* the sod?' cried Larkin in despair some months later.[27] Similarly, he felt enormous anxiety while *The North Ship* was being published and recorded ambivalence amounting to acute distress once it appeared. In the 1964 introduction to its reissue, Larkin described his initial reaction to the publisher's request to reissue the book – 'I was enormously flattered' (*RW*, 27). The publication date seemed to him to have been prolonged infinitely and agonisingly, and led in retrospect to a depth of emotion which seems out of proportion to the actual event: 'Then, as now, I could never contemplate it without a twinge, faint or powerful, of shame compounded with disappointment' (*RW*, 28). This suggests, again, how seriously he regarded these early evidences of his writing talent – and perhaps how much fervent hope he initially attached to them and to their success.

In later years, Larkin was characteristically wry about all three of these early books, denigrating both their value and his own literary ambitions at the time. He emphasised his lack of income from *The North Ship* and from *Jill*: one cup of tea with his publisher at Victoria Station was 'my sole payment for both books' (*RW*, 26). And he spoke of the publication of *Jill* (by the same publisher who had brought out *The North Ship*) as an almost freakish or ludicrous accident: 'I had rather despairingly bunged the novel at him, as no one else seemed interested' (*RW*, 26). On the reissue of *Jill* in 1964, he implored Barbara Pym to take no notice of the book: 'it's quite awful, don't pay any attention to it.'[28] His introduction to this edition of the novel reflects self-conscious detachment yet formidable defensiveness. Writing at length of the years which had elapsed since the book's composition, he concludes with a half apology: 'It will, I hope, still qualify for the indulgence traditionally extended to juvenilia' (*RW*, 24).

The appearance of these first three books confirmed to Larkin that he could publish; yet several years were to elapse before he published again and these took in the difficult period when he found he was unable to write a third novel. As to the reason he could not write the book, it is impossible to pin it to a single cause. The third novel, as he envisioned it in 1945, would be a sequel to the first two: as he wrote to Sutton, 'Now I am thinking of a third book in which the central character will pick up where Katherine left off and develop *logically* back to life again. In other words, the north ship will come back instead of being bogged up there in a glacier. Then I shall have finished this particular branch of soul-history (my own, of course) and what will happen then I don't know.'[29] Possibly he could not write the novel because he did not experience a figurative return from an emotional wilderness himself, and therefore could not describe it. After he went down from Oxford, the next few years found him struggling to come to grips with what course to pursue in relation to career, family life, and marriage; in personal as well as professional spheres, it was a period filled with several stresses. He moved several times in order to assume various library posts, and spent some time and effort studying for official library exams. While preparing for these in 1947, he wrote to Sutton that he intended to return to writing soon: 'I shall fling myself on my novel like a leopard on a piece of meat (or I hope I shall).'[30] Waiting for the results of the exams, he wrote again to Sutton about his doubts in relation to writing the novel: 'it is comical to see how little the writing of a book depends on technique – my present confusion is due to my not knowing quite what I feel or mean or want to put over. The trouble is, I suspect, I am trying to lift more than I can carry.'[31] The burden seemed to increase, as he wrote three months later: 'I have laid aside my work temporarily – or it has laid me aside, I'm not quite sure which.'[32] As in earlier bouts of difficulty in writing, when Larkin was bogged down in creating, he attempted to distance and depersonalise the task – and to become passive. The work itself is seen to have laid *him* aside rather than the other way around.

This is important because a pattern emerges in the way he saw himself and his work during this crucial period of transition. Between 1945 and 1955 he became a poet rather than a novelist (an unwilling transformation), a librarian rather than a writer, and he remained a bachelor rather than becoming a husband (a role which he contemplated somewhat anxiously, writing to Sutton in 1948 that 'marriage doesn't attract me, except as a refuge, and it ought to be more than that. I'm a let down all round').[33] What he seems to have been searching for in writing the unwritable third novel was sheer inspiration, or what he refers to as IMAGINATIVE POWER.[34] Yet the fascinating result of this period of not getting what he wanted – in not writing a novel – was that he managed to write poetry instead. And the imaginative power for this seems to have arrived by a circuitous route. He wrote the following to Sutton in 1950: 'there are some things you will not get because you want them so much – like missing an easy putt because the match depends on it. Agree? I can write poems now and again *because I want to write novels so badly*.'[35] (Again, the possibility of neurotic guilt acting to prevent the writing of novels could be considered. Although he read psychology avidly at the time, he seems not to have been able or willing to apply its insights to his own predicament – a task which would have been extremely difficult.)

Although Larkin said nothing to Sutton in his letters about the rejection of *In the Grip of Light*, it probably contributed to his general feeling of frustration in 1948–9. The fact that he did not mention it to his friend even suggests that he was ashamed of its having been turned down. (His emotional state at this time would also have been enormously affected by the death of his father in 1948. Later on, when he realised that he himself was dying at sixty-three, the same age as his father, he identified with him.) Nonetheless, a significant change in Larkin's writing occurred at this point of despair: he began to mock himself and to express his varied emotions more vividly in his poetry. And in achieving this feat, he employed some of the earlier strategies which he devised at Oxford – imitating other authors (he converted to Hardy's style of writing from Yeats'), and showing contempt for the reader, thus clearing a space for his own writing. In what was probably a less helpful reaction, he also continued to blame himself for allowing time to slip by, measuring his achievement in caustic terms. In October 1948, he wrote to Sutton: 'I calculated recently that since about 1946 I have written [love letters] sufficient to make up a novel about as long as *The Old Wives' Tale*. Do you think that is any consolation to me for having wasted three years? No: conserve your energy.'[36] Nonetheless, despite the contempt Larkin showered upon himself for lack of productivity, he fulfilled in another way the need he discerned in himself after finishing *A Girl in Winter*, when he wrote, 'I feel . . . that it's time I lived a bit. The furious creation of these last two years has spent itself and I must wait till the reservoir fills up again.'[37]

The transition which Larkin made from novelist to poet is interesting not only because it produced *The Less Deceived*, but because of his subsequent fierce emotional response to it. In some sense, he tried to recast the event and rewrite history; he created a huge joke of the ensuing situation in retrospect. In a 1979 interview, he described his initial reaction to the publication of *A Girl in Winter*:

> And I thought this was it, I'm made. But I could never write a third novel, though I must have spent about five years trying to. I felt a bit cheated. I'd had visions of myself writing 500 words a day for six months, shoving the result off to the printer and going to live on the Côte d'Azur, uninterrupted except for the correction of proofs. It didn't happen like that – very frustrating. (*RW*, 49)

This retelling of the story makes light of the ensuing dry period by exaggerating his ambitions – the dashing artist on the Côte d'Azur – and it foreshadows poetic counterparts to it which appear later in Larkin's poetry. His poem 'The Life with a Hole in it' pictures this same figure as:

> the shit in the shuttered château
> Who does his five hundred words
> Then parts out the rest of the day
> Between bathing and booze and birds
> (*CP*, 202)

Alas for the speaker's own dreams of glory, this possibility remains as 'far off as ever' (*CP*, 202). Similarly, the disappointed poet in 'Toads' becomes the unlucky chap who realises that he is unable to 'blarney' his way to 'getting / The fame and the girl and the money / All at one sitting' (*CP*, 90). At the same time, the fact that Larkin handles the rejection so lightly does not necessarily mean that it was easy to assimilate at the time; the anguish of a sense of personal failure still infuses his comments – and he seems to have felt a continuing need to bash someone, as he does by implying that the successful 'shit' in the château is just a 'shit'.

The main point here is that, according to his own lights, Larkin did not get what he wanted. His speculations about this period, much later in his life, describe an almost unwilling transformation as a writer: 'I wanted to "be a novelist" in a way I never wanted to "be a poet",' he told a *Paris Review* interviewer as late as 1982. The suggestion that he selfishly took the easy way out ('Was time a factor in choosing poetry over the novel form?') evoked a tart response: 'I wrote prose and poems equally from the age of, say fifteen. I didn't choose poetry: poetry chose me' (*RW*, 62). He was, in fact, writing prose and poetry equally in 1948, as evidenced by the fact that he sent out *In the Grip of Light* immediately following the publication of his two novels. But its subsequent rejection may ironically have confirmed his tendency to write poetry rather than fiction, since poetry provided the means of expressing the sense of failure which the rejection of the volume caused him to feel. He enabled himself to write the poetry composed during this period by complaining about the depression which made writing difficult for him.

Larkin's working notebook from 1944–1950 shows that he *was* writing poetry – even if it was poetry about not writing poetry. In doing this he was simply persevering, following the time-honoured tradition of making *kleine lieder* out of *schmerzen*, or songs out of sorrow. It is difficult to chart the progress of this transition in any definitive way, yet the poems which led up to this point tend to employ not only much of the imagery typical of *The North Ship*, but its general tone of romantic melancholy as well. Anthony Thwaite's edited version of the *Collected Poems* also indicates that Larkin composed a group of several poems between roughly April of 1946 and May of 1949 which tend to carry on in this same vein, without any noticeable or radical shift in style. 'Wedding-Wind', composed in September of 1946, is the first major exception to this kind of writing; as in *The North Ship*, most of the poems of this period tend to address subjects such as death, dreams, extreme distancing in love relationships, and cold and forbidding landscapes.

Still, by the time *The Less Deceived* appeared in 1955, the poetry has taken on a much more immediate and personal intensity, which suggests that some fairly distinctive change occurred at about 1949 – as the *Collected Poems* show, Larkin wrote at least five poems during the month of May in that year. One example of the shift in style between the two volumes can be seen by comparing two similar poems, 'To a Very Slow Air' (which was included in the collection *In the Grip of Light*) and 'Triple Time', which appeared in *The Less Deceived*. Both poems use strikingly similar imagery, which is transformed sharply in the later poem. 'To a Very Slow Air' contains phrases strongly reminiscent of poems in *The North Ship* having to do with nature, such as 'The golden sheep are feeding', in the first stanza and 'The cloven hills are kneeling' in the second (*CP*, 13). Nature here evokes joy in the poet, who articulates his response:

> Gladly my tongue praises
> This hour scourged of dissension
> By weight of their joyous fleeces.
> (*CP*, 13)

In 'Triple Time', landscape again appears as a central image in the poem, but it does so as a picture of despair and hopelessness connected to the poet's life cycle. He relates time, divided into past, present, and future, to particular locations, seen from various perspectives – the present appears as 'This empty street, this sky to blandness scoured,' yet also as the future which had been envisioned in childhood as 'Between long houses, under travelling skies' and containing 'An air lambent with adult enterprise' (*CP*, 73). Significantly, the present also appears (from a future perspective) in the guise of grazing sheep, an image which this poem shares with 'To a Very Slow Air'. When the present time appears to us in retrospect, it will be seen as:

> A valley cropped by fat neglected chances
> That we insensately forbore to fleece.
> (*CP*, 73)

In order to pinpoint how Larkin had changed his way of writing by the time he composed the later poem, we need to separate the elements of romanticism and irony in it; this is hard to do, but, roughly speaking, 'Triple Time' is different from its earlier counterpart because it seems more directly connected with the poet himself. It springs from Larkin's sense of despair and hopelessness. This is not to say that depression is the truest description of reality for him; but he interacts with nature in this poem in a meaningful way. The landscapes express his vision. 'To a Very Slow Air' records his response to nature, causing his tongue to "[praise] / This hour', while 'Triple Time' uses nature imagery in order to describe that which he innately knows and experiences (*CP*, 13). Also, the sheep in 'Triple Time' become metaphor, as they stand for disappointed hopes. In the same way, 'At Grass', an important transitional poem in this period which I return to later on, is also more far-reaching in its metaphors (the retired race-horses symbolise something about success and failure).

It is possible that this period of transition radically and permanently changed Larkin's style of writing, by channelling energy from an unwritable third novel into poetry which dealt – at least obliquely – with that frustration. More than providing merely a means of continuing to write during a time when he could find neither a literary voice nor a publisher, these poems about failure and despair significantly deepened his work. The 1948–9 poems in his working notebook reveal a fascinating progression which suggests a way in which Larkin might have fictionalised and thus distanced his griefs in his poetry. It is by no means the case that this group of poems contains only poems about personal failure; but they do tend to focus on problems related to creativity. On 4 April 1948, for instance, Larkin began the poem 'An April Sunday brings the snow', which concerns the death of his father. The poem describes the process of clearing up someone else's belongings, as the speaker finds himself moving about inside, 'shifting the store / Of jam you made of fruit' from the plum trees outside (*CP*, 21). The jars of jam symbolise in part their maker's inability to enjoy the fruits of his labours in the form of 'next summer's teas' (*CP*, 21). The poet concludes by musing on the finality of death:

> Behind the glass, under the cellophane,
> Remains your final summer – sweet
> And meaningless, and not to come again.
> (*CP*, 21)

This seems to suggest both a kind of wistful consolation and a warning – the work of creating can preserve and encapsulate a 'summer'. Yet it also appears in the end to comprise a 'meaningless' act; a sadness pervades the poem having to do with creative work as well as *memento mori* (*CP*, 21).

In the poems which follow on in Larkin's working notebook from 'An April Sunday brings the snow', a sense of tangible despair begins to emerge in a progressively more personal voice. On 18 May 1949, Larkin started the poem entitled 'To Failure', which begins to take stock of the enemy in a more wry and detached tone than that which the *North Ship* poems tend to employ; in its final version, the poem opens with lines which ironically undercut a heroic vision of the poet's defeat:

> You do not come dramatically, with dragons
> That rear up with my life between your paws
> And dash me butchered down beside the wagons,
> The horses panicking;
>
> (*CP*, 28)

Failure, he insists here, is dull. This may not be a specific reaction to his difficulties in writing at the time, and yet it does both particularise and address a pervading sense of despair, coming to grips with it more squarely than most of the *North Ship* poems seem to do. He gives shape and identity to his despair – as well as a certain dreary ordinariness. In an ironic stroke, the poet deliberately casts failure in the second stanza not as a fabulous, mythical beast, but as an irksome, tedious presence: 'It is these sunless afternoons, I find, / Instal you at my elbow like a bore' (*CP*, 28). This invokes an ironic description of the phenomenon rather than a romanticised one. It brings failure down to a more mundane level, as the poem concludes with a description of tedious banality: 'You have been here some time' (*CP*, 28). By making the depression seem less exalted, the poem also by implication makes it seem easier to address or possibly to alter that state. This poem is not especially more sombre and introspective than many in *The North Ship*. Still, 'To Failure' begins to make a subtle shift in perspective. Whereas the *North Ship* poems tend to be dramatic and lyrical in their fatalism, 'To Failure' is more flat and direct; yet it is accordingly more intense. Larkin begins here to attempt greater irony and also greater plainness; he moves figuratively from the 'gale-driven [birds]' of an early poem such as 'Within the dream you said' to 'toads' by way of dragons (*CP*, 299).

Closely connected to the shift toward expressing depression in less mystical terms is the strategy of lashing out at the cause of it – and thus gaining some greater distance or control. The possibility that Larkin may have felt the need to clear more space for his writing is suggested by the poem which follows next, a piece which is the earliest draft of a succession of variations on 'Fiction and the Reading Public'. In this satire he attempts to come to grips directly with the role of the reader in the writing process, and to assert himself as a writer against it. It expresses hostility towards the unappreciative, boorish reader, who demands cheap sensationalism:

Give me a thrill, says the reader,
Give me a kick;
I don't care how you succeed, or
What subject you pick.

(*CP*, 34)

The cause of greatest irritation is the reader's demand for a falsified (i.e. – optimistic) vision of life from the artist: 'But that's not sufficient, unless / You make me feel good' – a request impossible to comply with because this is a perspective which seems so far removed from Larkin's own experience (*CP*, 34). This poem thus marks another transition, one where Larkin begins a struggle with his feelings about writing which turns some of the blame outward, and thus releases him from some of the pressure of a critical audience. By pretending to despise and denounce the whole literary racket, he becomes able to gain some perspective on his sense of rejection and failure. Once he refuses the role of supplicant author, he can announce his independence; he no longer begs presses to publish his work and readers to put money in his pocket. He despises the lot.

This consciousness of failure or despair is taken up again in a following poem which turns the problem of creativity in another direction, and addresses the poet himself. The subject is still failure, but here the poet turns away from consciousness of the 'bore' at his elbow who represents failure, to a greater effort at analysis and at deciding what to do about it in response. He begins tentatively to take action and to contemplate the possibility of change. The poet admonishes himself in this poem not to desert art in the illusion that he can compensate for it in another way: 'Do not think to step from art's plain room / And lose your failure in more tolerant life. / Here failure will take longer, but will come.'[38] The moral he points out to himself is that failure is inevitable in either sphere; art and life are equally destructive. He concludes with a grim warning of inevitable doom: 'Whom art eludes, living exterminates.'[39] Though it is prescriptive and gloomy, the poet's response is also a fairly complex one, adducing an argument which implies both that he is not the guilty party (the muse is silent) and that he staunchly refuses to care anyway. Still, it also suggests an ability to move away from the paralysis of being always bothered by the 'bore' failure. It may be a convoluted way of forcing himself to continue to create art – after all, the poem consists largely of the direct threat of extermination if he abandons writing – but it nonetheless moves in some direction, and gains a new perspective on the problem of inability to write.

What appears from Larkin's pen next in this progression is 'At Grass', which seems suddenly to spring full-blown into being in Larkin's mature style.[40] 'At Grass' marks a definite turning point in its finely crafted style and lyricism which combine with Hardyesque plainness of diction and reverence for nature – and it also suggests that he had achieved a new way of seeing and writing about his emotional experience. In context of Larkin's working notebook, it appears during a time when the idea of personal failure seems to have preoccupied him. And though the poem does not directly address the subject of failed hopes, it leaps imaginatively to the other end of the spectrum: that of outliving one's success; he takes as his subject horses which have been turned out to pasture, and shows them tranquil and at rest. The racehorses appear to be at some distance from their days of glory, and from public notice. The crucial question raised is one of identity, and whether or not their fame will continue. The horses now stand 'anonymous again' after former days when 'their names were artificed / To inlay faded, classic Junes –' (CP, 29). The past confers a kind of immortality: 'Almanacked, their names live' because of their former victories (CP, 29). Yet in the end, they return to anonymity, again, in a way which seems graceful and elegant: 'they / Have slipped their names, and stand at ease' (CP, 29–30). The poem suggests that the horses can have a fruitful relationship with their fame although it is long past – largely by both accepting yet discounting it. Appearing first in the progression in which it does, this poem suggests a growing ability to see the problem of present decline and former glory from another angle. Larkin appears to have chosen a subject close to him and to have achieved a new and more thoughtful, diverse perspective on it. And he does so in a different mode from that which he generally uses in his first volume of poetry; less solemnity, moaning and self-pity cloud this piece.

Following the composition of 'At Grass', Larkin attains an increasingly detached, distanced view in his work. In the working notebook, he repeats and revises the satirical piece 'Fiction and the Reading Public' in still more belligerent versions. This line of approach appears to refresh his spirits so much that he repeats it periodically in salutary doses until the end of the writing notebook, which concludes in 1950. He keeps returning to the poem, to recopy it and add new revisions.[41] Another version of the piece appears again a few pages later in his notebook, invoking even more virulent, scathing denunciations of the insolent, philistine reader:

> For I call the tune in this racket:
> I pay your screw,
> Write reviews and balls on the jacket –
> So stop looking blue,

and so on.[42] This tone seems to hint at later satirical poems such as 'Study of Reading Habits' and 'Self's the Man', and it suggests tentative steps in that direction and away from the Yeatsian romanticism prevalent in *The North Ship*. Larkin does indeed complain against life in both kinds of poetry; yet in these manuscript poems he begins to give voice to his irritation with more shrillness and sheer volume.

Perhaps the most interesting example of this strain of satirical poems about literary reputation is an apologia which appears in late 1949 and early 1950. It is a long poem of several stanzas, alternately rewritten and revised through successive pages; it is largely an autobiographical piece which describes the poet's abandonment of the personified figure of 'Literature', and which explains his view of the awkward relationship which ensues between the two. In what is probably the earliest draft of this apologia, the elder figure is considerably less threatening to the poet than in his later manifestations. The first draft of the poem seems to be written in a self-consciously autobiographical manner, following the style of John Betjeman. Here Larkin creates a portrait of the artist as a young man, being lectured to by an older generation:

> But once, in my schooldays, an uncle arrived to see me:
> Sent to him, I found him leaning upon his stick,
> His broad black hat askew. '*Et ego* ...' he began,
> Gesturing about him.[43]

The uncle goes on to tell the young poet what and whom to write about – a fiddler in a restaurant seems to him suitable material –and warns him sombrely about the necessity for commitment and the discouragement which ensues from engaging in the 'bitter toil of art'. In this scheme, the figure of artistic judgement is strikingly patriarchal and prescriptive. The reference to '*Et in Arcadia ego*' could also constitute a kind of pun – either the older man recalls that he too once dwelled in Arcady, perhaps as a young lad in school, or he himself represents the reminder of the skull of death. In either variation, his presence seems rather oppressive and sinister, so much so as to overwhelm the poet himself.

In later versions of the poem, however, the uncle is transformed into the even more forbidding and generalised figure of personified 'Literature', and the poet begins to speak more forthrightly in response. These later versions of the poem focus more on the poet's relationship with the forbidding elder, thus bringing the conflict more into the centre of the poem, and describing his sense of discomfort and his avoidance. The last and best of these is a fascinating piece on several counts. The poem describes a particular character – again, the older patriarch who represents Art or Literature – more vividly than any of Larkin's previous work. Furthermore, the poet carries on from the irritation which he vented in 'Fiction and the Reading Public' and begins to express forceful, positive hatred and denunciation, through dramatising his own constraint, disappointment, and frustration. Rather than accepting the criticism of the elder man, however, the poet here begins to fight back, first by determining not to talk to him at all and then by insisting on his own point of view.

This anger is evident in the opening of the poem, where the poet describes various near encounters with 'Literature', whom he deliberately avoids meeting: 'When I see Literature / I turn down a side street, squashing my hat down lower. / A meeting would be awkward.'[44] The poem goes on to examine the causes of this division in a defensive way. The poet insists that the separation was inevitable and involuntary: 'For we are no longer friends: / There's been no quarrel – he's far too good-natured.' The explanation offered is that the two simply '"don't see eye to eye;" / Our interests have diverged.'[45] In effect, the poet seems to be attempting to understand why he cannot (or will not) write anymore. Significantly, he declines to blame himself for the silence. He seems here, in contrast to preceding poems about abandoning art for life, to refuse self-chastisement and thus to obtain a superior moral position with respect to his enemy. Further, he begins to take the offensive, declaring later that he despises 'Literature': 'Well, I hate him, / at least; put that down for a start.'[46]

Most innovative of all in this progression, Larkin reverses the usual situation of supplicant artist in search of his muse by making literature seek out the poet – albeit in a characteristically uncaring and casual way. The figure of Literature appears in one version of the poem in the guise of a clergyman, who possesses a jovial yet insinuating air and a 'fine popular-preacher's head.'[47] He accosts the poet with cries that he has not seen him for some time, and shows incomprehension and concern at the news that the poet is no longer

writing, declaring at the end of the dialogue, '"We must talk about
this."' The poet's excuses for not writing are summarily put aside:
'"Don't tell me you're simply sulking: / We shan't allow that."' Yet
the cause of this abandonment strikes a more philosophical note, and
reveals at least one perspective on the poet's part, speaking as an
artist. He defends himself against the charge of not writing with a
traditional kind of argument: life seems to him to be '"much more
serious"' than art.[48] Yet clearly, despite Literature's alleged concern,
the two will never meet to discuss the matter further. And it is not
because, as the poet has been claiming, he himself has elaborately
avoided contact with the great man, which adds to his bitterness.
Their actual conversation reveals that Literature wishes only to
reproach the recalcitrant artist, and not to help him or to define the
source of the difficulty. The poet's frustration results from the fact
that he is cajoled, harangued – and fundamentally ignored. In
response, the poet returns home and meditates on a vision of the city
outside his window. This seems an inconclusive reaction in that it
continues to place him in the position of an artist who is isolated; he
is separated from life, which remains outside the window, while he
in turn observes it from a detached position rather than participating
in it. This gesture anticipates several similar attitudes in Larkin's
poetry, such as the willed solitude which appears in 'Reasons for
Attendance' from *The Less Deceived*, in which the poet chooses
solitude as necessary for the creation of art.

The poem thus suggests that the artist's relationship to the figure
of 'Literature' is deeply ambivalent – and that he did not expect it to
be so. To his fury, the poet is simultaneously ignored, frustrated, and
reproached in a way which seems to reflect a struggle with the
creative process. As part of a series of similar pieces, it also implies
that once again Larkin was able to continue writing in a difficult
time by taking up the subject of *not* writing.

The poem continues from this description of inner turmoil on the
part of the poet to a further tirade against the literary marketplace
and a renunciation of the pursuit of art, which recall the charges
made in the earlier poem 'Fiction and the Reading Public'. The poet
expresses rage at the literary world, denouncing fame as shallow
and critics as haughty; he rails against the 'stench of success'.[49] A
long passage on this subject includes a dialogue between several men
sitting at their club, who evaluate various authors of their
acquaintance and find all of them wanting in some respect:

This Athenaeum Club of ravaged and photographed faces.

'Old Blank is a master – but somehow he just misses *greatness.*'
Young Dotted-Line-passion, I grant you: oh, temper and fire –
But hardly the tone of greatness: while old Empty Barrel –
Tragedy, poignance, humour, philosophy too –
But one of the great? I doubt it . . . *so* pessimistic![50]

This passage is peculiarly effective because it hints at another reason
besides writer's block for an artist's hesitation to write – though he
might be able to write and even to publish, he may be dismissed as
being limited in scope and ability. Although this audience seems
more sophisticated and discriminating than that in 'Fiction and the
Reading Public', who simply wants cheap thrills, the moral here
seems to be that superior judges are not to be trusted either.

This means of attack – vilifying the enemy – seems a clever
psychological strategy. Larkin denigrates the fame for which he
yearns by devaluing its audience and mocking that audience's ability
to judge. If he paints the literary 'racket' as worthless, it lessens the
pain of not attaining fame or success in conventional terms. Thus he
can reject it loudly – and he can go on writing on his own terms,
with disregard for the vulgar throng. This series of poems which
addresses the subject of failure seems to have worked to good effect.
The notebook shows Larkin going on to write 'Deceptions' (also a
poem about victimisation and grief, which are related themes) and
several other poems (including a repeat and expansion of 'Fiction
and the Reading Public', which seems to suggest that another dose
of self-assertion was required). Through a long process of
internalising and expressing his general sense of failure at the time,
he seems to have begun to write more directly, more personally –
with less abstraction and with more anger. This focuses his work
more. The poems which record the process of attaining this
increased irony are not especially promising in themselves, but they
seem to have served as a transition through which his writing gained
more vigour, authority and intensity. Larkin seems to have regarded
them more as exercises than as promising early drafts; most of them
he did not publish. They were useful as a transition; he wrote them
and moved on.

Success did not, of course, follow immediately upon composition
or publication of 'At Grass' and the other poems completed at this
period. This spate of 1949 poems led to private publication and
circulation of *XX Poems* in 1951, which failed to attract notice.[51] *The
Less Deceived* was refused by one press before it was solicited by
George and Jean Hartley and accepted in 1954, to appear in 1955. An

unpublished poem in Larkin's post-1948 folder of poems illustrates some of his continuing frustration about writing at the time. 'The Literary World', takes up the subject of one of Franz Kafka's periods of writer's block. The speaker compares Kafka's period of inability to write – five months – with his own, concluding grimly that Kafka should be forced to endure the poet's own dry period of five years: 'Then you'll know about depression' (*CP*, 38). At the same time, in writing about a subject such as writer's block which vexed, wounded and annoyed him, Larkin began at this juncture to forge a distinctive, ingenious sort of pessimism.

One related aspect of this transition in style of writing is Larkin's penchant during the decade as a whole for reading Lawrence and Freud, and his attempt to come to terms with the role of tapping one's emotions in the course of creating. He admired Lawrence enormously for his passion, writing to Sutton: 'no good writer (i.e. – DHL [sic] is afraid of his emotion.'[52] (Ironically, he later virtually abandoned his admiration for Lawrence altogether, at least in public. In the same *TLS* survey in which Larkin declared Pym's novels to be 'underrated', he strenuously declared *Women in Love* to be much 'overrated'.)[53] Further, Larkin attempted to analyse himself in light of what he learned from both writers, describing himself early on at Oxford as follows: 'my particular form of neurosis is being afraid of all emotions, and of trying to suppress them.' He goes on to suggest a direct link with the creative process, proclaiming that 'It is this reason that stops me from being a writer.'[54] This conclusion, which he reached in 1941, was still exercising Larkin in 1948, when he wrote again to Sutton: 'I have gone on fuddling my head with psychological books and now figure myself as every kind of neurotic.'[55]

Part of this fear was simply that he could do nothing about his psychological make-up. No cure was possible, even though insight could be achieved. Along with several other undergraduates at Oxford, Larkin was reading *Sons and Lovers* and drawing conclusions that horrified him. He confided to Sutton at one point, some years later, 'I wonder if I am tied to my mother?'[56] The major effect of such a situation would be the block that this would pose to his writing, since it suggests 'emotions being all engaged out of sight below,' and indeed, this statement is accompanied in the letter by a cartoon of a man up to the waist in water, with an octopus wrapping its tentacles around his legs.[57] Mostly, the thought infuriates him because of his perceived helplessness: 'How irritating! And nasty, too! for I always conceive an ailment like that as resembling some very submarine tendrils of oneself having fastened onto some object and which one can't get them to release by any effort of will.'[58] Perhaps this is a reductive view to take; but it does show a tendency to self-examination which finds its way into the poetry as well. If Larkin saw himself as being excessively afraid of emotion, he also tried to write about how he felt. The poem 'Neurotics', for instance (written in March or April of 1949), is fairly impersonal and distanced – the neurotic in question is referred to as 'you', rather than 'I' – and yet it attempts to describe his state of hopelessness and isolation:

> No one gives you a thought, as day by day
> You drag your feet, clay-thick with misery.
> (*CP*, 22)

The main point is that of inability to change: 'The mind, it's said, is free: / But not your minds' (*CP*, 22). Yet this poem, like the other transitional ones composed in May of 1949, shows Larkin trying to come to grips with something central in himself. Rather than distancing his feelings and placing them out in nature, he turns to his own situation and describes a tangible sense of internal misery.

As Larkin himself remarked, the phenomenon of creating art out of pain is by no means unusual. He observes that for him, unhappiness 'provokes a poem' (*RW*, 47). Naturally he wrote about failure as a common human experience; still, as all artists do, he struggled with the proper manner in which to regard and to evaluate his own work throughout his career. His response to his increasing fame seems to embody a conflicting variety of moods. In one sense, he was extravagantly disappointed about the course of his writing career. He commiserated with Barbara Pym about feeling unproductive, finding it appalling to be 'over 50 and "nothing done," as I feel.'[59] Also, the severe writer's block which he experienced after the publication of *High Windows* in 1974 shows that he could not always pull out of it easily – or indeed, at all, during the last few years of his life. Poetry itself seems to have faded for him; he wrote gloomily to Pym in 1975: 'In fact I feel somewhat in the doldrums these days: of course, *work* goes on, but I am quite unable to do anything in the evenings – the notion of expressing sentiments in short lines having similar sounds at their ends seems as remote as mangoes on the moon.'[60] The exasperation, the anxiety, the edginess to create was indeed a struggle, and continued to be so until poetry dried up for Larkin altogether and became, in his words to John Betjeman, 'as remote as the prayers of medieval Chinese monks.'[61]

In sum, Larkin's creative process throughout his literary career seems fraught with difficulty, yet marked with intense determination to write. The rejection of *In the Grip of Light* in 1948, compounded by his inability to write a third novel, seems in the end to have acted as a catalyst, producing still better work; and the major shift in literary influence from Yeats to Hardy, which facilitated this change during the 1945–55 decade, had a lasting effect on his poetry. Hardy's example called for a more immediate, colloquial, personal style, which Larkin subsequently embraced. At the same time, Larkin's growing sense of sharpness and irony did not entirely preclude his earlier romantic tendencies. Recent scholarly work by Andrew Motion and Terry Whalen, among others, reminds us that Larkin's symbolist sympathies were to some extent merely submerged in *The Less Deceived*, not eradicated entirely. Whalen comments: 'The most unhelpful critical reaction to Larkin's move from an early romantic impulse to a "less deceived" maturity has been a tendency amongst critics to overstate the pendulum's swing.'[62] Motion also points to symbolist influence evident in Larkin's later work, adding: 'His original admiration for the heroic, aspiring, self-dramatising characteristics of Yeats was not completely dispelled as his sympathy for the humbler manner of the English line developed: it was restrained and made to perform a crucial role in the creation of his mature style.'[63]

At the same time, this decade-long period of transformation remains significant because it resulted in the first notable manifestation of Larkin's own characteristic style – one which was to have a great effect in restoring and revitalising this peculiarly 'English line', and which was neither Yeats nor Hardy speaking, but Larkin himself. Figuratively writing himself into failure in the late 1940s, he seems to have written himself out again with willed determination. 'A good poem about failure is a success,' as Larkin once remarked, and in the complex creative process, even an unsuccessful poem can have its uses (*RW*, 74).

2

The Lyrical Poems

Distance and detachment from nature

While numerous other events played a part in Larkin's dramatic
stylistic development between *The North Ship* and *The Less Deceived*,
the respective literary influences of Yeats and Hardy remain crucial
to that change, both because Larkin saw them as significant and
because their distant presences also point to an underlying
romanticism in his work. Yeats and Hardy loomed large in his
consciousness, yet their effects on his poetry were quite different.
The most important difference is that Larkin imitated Yeats in a
fairly direct way, admitting that he had been swept away by Yeats'
music, and appropriating the images as well as the romantic and
melancholy tone of his early Celtic period. Yeats' rhetoric caught
his imagination to such a degree that *The North Ship* often appears to
be a Yeatsian pastiche, an exercise in imitating another poet's work
which extends even to the borrowing of particular lines.[1] This close
identification with another writer in part stems from Larkin's
impressionable (artistic) age at the time he first encountered Yeats'
work, and from his general way of writing at the time; as a young
poet and novelist at Oxford, Larkin imitated several writers in turn,
and constantly measured his own literary achievement against
theirs. The literary apprenticeship which he undertook in service to
Yeats seems especially notable because it heavily marks the first
volume of Larkin's which saw print, and therefore his readers tend
to regard Yeats' influence as paramount in Larkin's development.
Moreover, as Larkin points out, there is a further reason for the
obvious nature of this close connection between the two poets;
Yeats' influence, he argues, is almost overwhelming: 'In fairness to
myself it must be admitted that his is a particularly potent music,
pervasive as garlic, and has ruined many a better talent' (*RW*, 29).

One would not expect Hardy's influence to have affected Larkin
in this same way, since Larkin was already established as a poet and

had achieved more authority in his writing by the time he began to
admire Hardy's work; he had gone down from Oxford, found a job,
and begun to publish. At the same time, Hardy's influence was
unique; it acted largely as a counterbalance to what had gone
before. It seemed important in drawing him away from Yeats' style
as well as in establishing an alternative model to follow. And the
extent of this influence was perhaps overstated in retrospect, as it
seems to have been altered slightly in Larkin's varying accounts. In
the Preface to *The North Ship*, Larkin casts the change in his style as
due to a definite conversion to Hardy, heralded by the presence of
the little blue poetry volume next to his bedside. In yet another
version of the story, given a few years later in an interview, he
speaks of the change in more general terms:

> At the end of the war I began reading Hardy's poetry without any
> great thought of him as an influence. Indeed he wasn't an influence at
> all formally. With Hardy it was more the spirit of the man, the
> feeling, which is as defiable [sic] as the subject-matter and as broad.
> After that Yeats came to seem so artificial – all that crap about masks
> and Crazy Jane and all the rest. It all rang so completely unreal.[2]

According to this rendition, Hardy's contribution was as much by
example as by precept: his work encouraged Larkin to trust in his
own feelings and to write about them.

A further distinction to be made between these kinds of
influences was that the plain 'English line' in Larkin's work, which
Andrew Motion traces back through Hardy, Tennyson and
Wordsworth, derives in part from romanticism.[3] And this strain
stems from the Yeatsian influence as well as the Hardyesque one,
although in a more exotic form. As Larkin himself points out, the
aspect of Yeats' work which he imitated was not the modernist
strain of Byzantium, masks, madness and political issues, but the
early, Celtic mysticism, which Yeats in turn learned as a young poet
from Morris, Rosetti, and the other Pre-Raphaelite poets. The most
immediate effect of Yeats on Larkin's poetry is the romanticism
which appears prominently in *The North Ship*; and it is easily
discernible as an influence. This is not to say that Hardy's influence
cannot be felt in Larkin's work – the churchyard in 'Church Going',
for instance, shows some affinities with Hardy's settings. Hardy's
pessimism might have appealed to Larkin's sensibilities as well, and
might have encouraged him to express his own melancholy in a less
grand manner. And Hardy's influence perhaps also encouraged

Larkin to embrace a deliberately anachronistic taste in poetry, as exemplified in his comment about being asked to judge a poetry contest, and inquiring 'Where are all the love poems? And nature poems? And they said, Oh, we threw all those away. I expect they were the ones I should have liked' (*RW*, 76).

Most important, Hardy's influence might have shown Larkin that he could dramatise his separation from nature in a stance of brooding melancholy, rather than following Yeats' restless seeking after union with it. His departure from Yeats' influence can be seen in his poems which represent the way in which he perceives and deals with nature; and much of this has to do with romantic sensibilities which are then made ironic, as he describes his detachment from nature and love.

In some sense all that changes is Larkin's diction; the romantic subject matter goes underground, or is clothed in different descriptive terms. As critics have observed, Larkin's Hardyesque side continued through his work along with a symbolist tendency, which then re-emerged again more plainly in *High Windows*; yet these may be more closely meshed in Larkin's individual style than is usually allowed.

An example of this romantic irony is the image that recurs throughout Larkin's work of the poet sitting or lying inside a room, while nature moves restlessly outside. This is a striking image because the poet is separated from nature by being enclosed away from it, although he nonetheless remains acutely conscious of it. It is as though the pathetic fallacy (nature reflecting man's emotions) has been expressed at one remove; the poet alludes to nature's connection with his own feelings from inside a building rather than from outside in nature. Moreover, his position of being aware of but distant from nature illustrates the dilemma he experiences of yearning for transcendence – or union with something outside himself – and yet being denied it.

Larkin's early poems often create a particular setting for the poet to reflect on his own emotional state, in which he is isolated from nature. These take the form of bitter 'aubades', such as 'Dawn', where he wakes to 'hear a cock / Out of the distance crying', and to look out of the window and 'see the clouds flying' (*CP*, 248). These events in nature parallel and give expression to his own experience of loneliness: 'How strange it is / For the heart to be loveless, and as cold as these' (*CP*, 284). The poet here stresses his consciousness of nature outside. The consideration of the poet himself – or of his 'heart' – comes at the end; upon first waking, the poet pays attention to outside sounds and sights. These are central to his perception of, or description of, his own state of mind.

This consciousness of nature works in a similar way in 'Ugly Sister', where the speaker ascends to her room and lies down on the bed. Once there, her first action is to remove all other distractions: 'Let the music, the violin, cornet and drum / Drowse from my head' (CP, 292). This clears the way for focused concentration on nature outside – again, it is perceived from inside that room on that bed: 'I will attend to the trees and their gracious silence, / To winds that move' (CP, 292). This seems a willed switch *to* nature images *from* musical ones. The reason for this stems from a lack of love, and possibly provides a substitution for it or a new perspective on this lack. The speaker was not 'bewitched in adolescence / And brought to love', and therefore she will turn to the sounds of nature (trees and wind) (CP, 292). This poem and the later ones which recreate this scene show a simultaneous detachment from, yet connection to, nature outside. The title of this poem suggests that the 'Ugly Sister' is a hermit-like creature, possibly even an outcast, and she becomes one of the first of Larkin's protagonists to take refuge from society in this way.

Nature imagery recurs often in *The North Ship*, usually in recognisable Yeatsian images. Yet what is distinctive is its unvarying perception of the outside world; in all of these poems, nature is depicted as cold (and thus alienating) *and* as in powerful motion. In various poems, the wind is often 'deafening', there is 'Dawn coming, and rain / Driving across a darkening autumn', and the wind 'runs wild'. (CP, 301, 293). In another poem, a dream reveals the wind as a malevolent force: 'the wind climbed up the caves / To tear at a dark-faced garden' (CP, 267). Nature in this Yeatsian terrain is full of heaving motion, and dawn brings 'A weariness of daybreak' (CP, 289). There are often trees and wind and sounds, as in 'Night Music': 'At one the wind rose, / And with it the noise / Of the black poplars' (CP, 300). The effect of nature's power and occasional malevolence on the poet is not addressed in many of these poems, though it creates an appropriate setting for their descriptions of disillusionment.

In several poems, however, nature provides a direct correlation to the poet's emotions. The poem 'Kick up the fire, and let the flames break loose' in particular dramatises his loneliness. The poet strives to keep his evening guest in his rooms. Accordingly, he '[drives] the shadows back' and '[Prolongs] the talk on this or that excuse' (CP, 285). The poem vividly describes the terror of loneliness;

the guest's departure into the outside world causes figurative death, and brings 'instantaneous grief' (*CP*, 285). Yet the poem depicts this aloneness partly in terms of the movement of nature outside the room. The street is 'windy', and the night only momentarily 'comes to rest / While some high bell is beating two o'clock' (*CP*, 285). This poem makes clear the connection between being inside and conscious of nature – and the loneliness this can engender. Larkin does not point out this 'grief' of separation in every case, but this poem seems a precursor of '*Vers de Société*' and other subsequent poems where solitude necessarily results in loneliness. The accompanying sense of loss of a particular 'guest' or person becomes submerged but remains present in later poetry through nature's restlessness outside.

In the poetry following *The North Ship*, Larkin elaborated on the theme of separation from nature because it best expressed the pessimistic, Hardyesque element in his poetry (disillusionment with nature's indifference) while at the same time retaining some of his earlier Yeatsian romantic sensibility. When through a 'conversion' to Hardy he decided that it was impractical – or impossible – to become exalted, connected or merged with nature, he still continued to dramatise the fact of his isolation from it. In his later, post-Yeatsian work, Larkin tends to stay inside buildings. His distinctive sense of spiritual revelation often occurs while he is indoors looking outside, as in 'Waiting for breakfast, while she brushed her hair', which places the poet inside a hotel room looking outside: 'I looked down at the empty hotel yard / Once meant for coaches' (*CP*, 20). The poem describes the advent of a kind of spiritual revelation, as he alters his earlier perception of 'Featureless morning, featureless night'. This ordinariness is pronounced a 'misjudgment', and he moreover receives not only love ('Turning, I kissed her, / Easily for sheer joy tipping the balance to love'), but a 'tender visiting', accompanied by a poignant sense of awe and wonder (*CP*, 20). This poem, he claims, is representative of his move away from Yeats' influence, and 'though not noticeably better than the rest, shows the Celtic fever abated and the patient sleeping soundly' (*RW*, 30). It heralds the later poetry in which the poet's relationship with nature changes subtly, becoming less exalted. In 'Waiting for breakfast . . . ' the vision which appears seems more like the harsh bell of Art which sounds later in 'Reasons for Attendance', or at least is separate from nature and seems to call for the poet's separation, as the closing lines of 'Waiting for breakfast . . . ' formulate it: 'Will you refuse to come till I have sent / Her terribly away, importantly live / Part invalid, part baby, and part saint?' (*CP*, 20). At the same time, throughout succeeding work, the separation which the poet feels from nature remains – it has largely followed him inside as he peers out of a window or lies on a bed contemplating its existence. And he continually reworks images of enclosure yet consciousness of outside, which underline his pessimism and irony.

There is compelling evidence of his sense of isolation from the world around him in the fact that even when the poet is not alone, and is in bed with a lover, it is still the outside world that holds most importance for him. This forms the basis for 'The bottle is drunk out by one' from *The North Ship*. This time love has happened *on* the bed, though it creates only a brief and superficial sense of union. The lovers now 'lie apart', after a perfunctory act: 'Love and its commerce done' (*CP*, 277). More than merely an expression of *post coitum triste*, the depression recorded here reflects infinite loneliness. The poet primarily considers the passing hours through the night, his sleeplessness, his utter exhaustion, and the winds outside. Most of his reverie has to do with things which exist outside the room, both in present and future; the poet not only considers the winds and dark during the night, but he '[waits] for morning, and the birds', and the sound of footsteps and voices outside in the street (*CP*, 277). His disillusionment – even his conception of reality – becomes projected outside the room.

'Talking in Bed', from *The Whitsun Weddings*, repeats many of the same images which appear in 'The bottle is drunk out by one'. The primary scene of both poems is a bed, where two lovers lie together; and in 'Talking in Bed' the poet is also acutely conscious of the setting beyond the room:

> Outside, the wind's incomplete unrest
> Builds and disperses clouds about the sky,
>
> And dark towns heap up on the horizon.
> None of this cares for us.
>
> (*CP*, 129)

This later poem, however, differs from the earlier one in two crucial ways. First of all, the poet explicitly comments on the lovers' relationship to the outside world, stressing its indifference: 'None of this cares for us' (*CP*, 129). This suggests that he wants something from the world, or that he feels isolated from it in some way that he regrets; and that the power of the outside world is ironically insubstantial, as the towns are as easily moved or shifted as the clouds are. Second, the poem also addresses the question of the lovers' relation to each other. The poet goes on to contradict the assumption of sadness by saying that he is at a 'unique distance from isolation' – this is so because, of course, he is lying in bed with someone (*CP*, 129). Still, this phrase evokes the distinction between loneliness and aloneness without directly stating it. He is only not alone (*CP*, 129). It also points to an anti-romantic kind of disillusionment, arising from the lovers' increasing difficulty in communicating. The beginning of the poem implies this by suggesting what should be yet is not, thus contrasting appearance to reality:

> Talking in bed ought to be easiest,
> Lying together there goes back so far,
> An emblem of two people being honest.
> (CP, 129)

This becomes a pun in a couple of ways; the lovers may be 'lying' (not speaking the truth) to each other, and they may be 'Lying together' in a sexual sense. It is a paradox, since lying cannot be an emblem of honesty. This growing estrangement results in increasing silence, which in turn seems to lead to consciousness of the presence of nature beyond the room.

The outside world becomes important in this situation because the poet looks to it for answers: 'Nothing shows why' the lovers cannot be both honest and loving. They confront a cosmic indifference which they cannot overcome or palliate. At the same time it is 'difficult to find / Words at once true and kind, / Or not untrue and not unkind' (*CP*, 129). The clouds in the sky and towns on the horizon have no care for the couple, and no explanation for them; they neither 'care' nor 'show why' in the same way that the two in bed cannot find words that are kind and true, or, in the futher qualification of a double negative, not actually harmful through either dishonesty or meanness: 'not untrue and not unkind' (*CP*, 129). But in addition, the restless outside world of wind and movement creates a situation in which the lovers would ordinarily be isolated, because they are not a part of it – they are in a room on a bed. Therefore the clouds and towns contribute to a sense of 'isolation' which the couple can in turn distance *themselves* from by being together and thus at a 'unique distance from isolation' (though this too is unfulfilling) (*CP*, 129). This vivid sense of nature outside emphasises the poet's inability to relate to the world at large – and to attain truth or oneness with his lover. It becomes a significant background for the more immediate problem of their fragmented love.

Ironically, within Larkin's scheme, the way to solve this difficulty with personal relationships is to be not conscious. Another couple who also lie together appear in 'An Arundel Tomb'. The earl and countess are frozen into their poses; they 'lie in stone', yet they attain some lasting communion, as his hand is 'holding her hand' (*CP*, 110). This becomes an emblem of an extremely positive kind, as the end of the poem posits that their union proves 'Our almost-instinct almost true: / What will survive of us is love' (*CP*, 111). Yet as several critics have pointed out, the optimistic element here is problematic.[4] The two 'almosts' in these last lines both qualify the assertion (it is only an 'almost-instinct' and only 'almost' proven true), yet they also make it seem more likely a good thing because it is qualified, and thus not facile. And the union does profoundly affect the viewer, who sees 'with a sharp tender shock, / His hand withdrawn, holding her hand' (*CP*, 110).

Still, the nature of the couple's union is problematic. In fact, like the couple in 'Talking in Bed', they are close to lying in the sense of being dishonest: 'Time has transfigured them into / Untruth' (*CP*, 111). The poet says that their 'stone fidelity' is something that 'They hardly meant' and therefore it is in part a kind of accident, rather than something consciously chosen (*CP*, 111). This qualifies the hopeful aspect of the poem. The gesture is in a way a pretend or throwaway grace – 'faithfulness in effigy' suggests permanence, perhaps, but largely in an aesthetic or even accidental sense (*CP*, 110). Further, the poet comments that it cannot be what the earl and countess would have chosen or expected, as they looked to an imminent resurrection which has not yet occurred: 'They would not think to lie so long' (*CP*, 110). The image of love certainly does survive in them, though technically it was the sculptor who conferred this gesture on them.

As in the poems discussed earlier in this light, the outside world becomes important in relation to the stationary people inside. The earl and countess, and the church in which the tomb lies, are set in context of cyclical nature existing outside and perceived through windows and at a distance: 'Snow fell, undated. Light / Each summer thronged the glass' (*CP*, 110). Nature continues in its round outside, a fact which emphasises the couple's persistence and sameness through time. Nature both continues to change and remains the same in its unvarying pattern of seasons. At the same time, a succession of visitors comes to see the tomb through the centuries; but by contrast, they are changed: 'And up the paths / The endless altered people came' (CP, 110). Man's history has changed through time in a way in which nature's pattern has not – snow and light continue to be the same, while the entire structure of society has altered. The 'old tenantry' have been turned away, and modern visitors cannot read the Latin names on the tomb (CP, 110).

'An Arundel Tomb' presents a public emblem of love and fidelity which recreates in idealised form the lying together of 'Talking in Bed'. Both couples are framed in context of – and to some extent affected by – the outside world, which continues on its own round of seasons and which does not affect them, but stays at a remote distance. These two poems depict poignant situations of 'almost' and what 'ought' to be but is not – kindness and truth, 'talking in bed', glorious resurrection. Neither the brave fidelity of both couples nor their unique distance from isolation contravenes the bleakness of their frozen isolation from nature through time.

The most striking sense of division between inside and outside settings appears in 'The Building', where enclosure is portrayed as frightening. The building itself symbolises a kind of prison: the hospital contains 'rooms and rooms past those' which comprise an increasing succession of isolations (CP, 192). This contrasts with the freedom of movement which is possible outside, which is addressed in a romantic apostrophe:

> O world,
> Your loves, your chances, are beyond the stretch
> Of any hand from here!
>
> (CP, 192)

'The Building' transforms this sense of duality between the outside world and inside building into a sinister division. For much of the poem, the speaker looks out of the window at life outside as evidencing a kind of natural supernaturalism. It is a miracle that the world exists. Ordinary events become extremely significant, as a result, creating a world

> Where kids chalk games, and girls with hair-dos fetch
>
> Their separates from the cleaners –
>
> (CP, 192)

Likewise, the fortunate ones are those who can escape imprisonment in the most mundane way possible, and walk 'Out to the car park, free' (*CP*, 192).

As the title suggests, the action of the poem largely occurs inside. Much of 'The Building' is concerned with describing the environment of the hospital; and the speaker increases the reader's sense of anxiety by returning again and again to the waiting room. This remains the focal point; a limbo where one waits to be called in order to climb to one's 'appointed [level]' (*CP*, 191). The poet might turn and survey the outside ('For the moment, wait, / Look down at the yard'), but he invariably returns inside to the consciousness of the patients' passivity (*CP*, 192). The poem heightens this dialectic between the two places by the closing, which depicts visitors streaming into the hospital, bearing 'wasteful, weak, propitiatory flowers' (*CP*, 193). The final movement described is in the direction of inside, a progression into a building whose size suggests not power or efficiency, but rather an inverse proportion of these; the hugeness of the 'error' it attempts to correct (*CP*, 191).

The sense of a confining enclosure, as portrayed in 'The Building', appears again in Larkin's work in a broader sense as well. Just as Mr Bleaney's room is a kind of coffin ('one hired box' to measure the man who lives there), the hospital building also prefigures death, containing as it does wards full of patients in beds, ironically described in terms of saints in heaven: upstairs are 'The unseen congregations whose white rows / Lie set apart above' (*CP*, 103, 192). The building remains symbolic of illness and death: its powers cannot '[contravene] / The coming dark' (*CP*, 193). And yet if Larkin is to some extent a suburban poet, he remains something of a romantic also, especially in poems such as 'Coming', where the 'serene / Foreheads of houses' and the song of a thrush awaken a childlike perspective almost amounting to joy (*CP*, 33). He shows no particular interest in architecture or in types or styles of buildings – they are usually generalised settings which are unimportant in themselves. Yet it is significant that his melancholy contemplation of nature often occurs from inside, which emphasises man's isolation from nature.

The poet often makes a sharp distinction between nature outside and man's enclosure inside a building, a scene which dramatises man's separation from nature. 'Church Going' seems to alter this habitual consciousness of nature by focusing initially on the inside of a building to the exclusion of its surroundings. The poet begins his encounter with the church building by describing the contents of the building; but the distinctions between what is outside in nature and what is inside in man's architectural dominion begin to blur. The building is seen by the poet as surrounded by the forces of nature and perhaps soon to be merged with them. He imagines the decaying building being eventually let 'rent-free to rain and sheep'; thus nature itself will enter the church and become part of it, or simply take it over completely (CP, 97). The destructive forces of nature are even now merging with the elements of the building: 'Grass, weedy pavement, brambles, buttress, sky' all coalesce (CP, 98). These increasingly nullify the church and its function, making of it 'A shape less recognisable each week, / A purpose more obscure' (CP, 98). Plants grow up in the cracks ('weedy pavement'), and the church building is gradually merging entirely with its surroundings (CP, 98).

In fact, the larger setting of the building becomes almost as important as the church itself. The poet sees it as 'A serious house on serious earth', and as existing on a symbolic 'cross of ground' (CP, 98). These references to the churchyard tend to make it seem that nature has some potential religious significance as well, at least as it is set apart from the unattractive 'suburb scrub' surrounding it (CP, 98).

Religion remains ambiguous or undefinable, though, either through an inherent lack in the church's ability to communicate its value or in the poet's own lack of comprehension. In some sense, the church building - which also contains some aspects of nature - becomes the all-important setting which the poet must interpret, much as the romantic poets went outside to learn nature's moral lessons from vernal woods. Characteristically, Larkin's speaker feels isolated from this setting, both in its reference to nature and to religion. The basic problem, as the poet defines it, is that he doesn't know 'what to look for' (CP, 97). Does the meaning of the church reside in the historical past ('it held unspilt / So long and equably what since is found / Only in separation'), or in the still existing symbols of its spiritual function in worship (the 'parchment, plate and pyx' which he imagines salvaged from the decaying buildings and with them put 'on show') (CP, 98, 97)? He tries to answer this question by wondering what kind of person will be 'the last, the very last, to seek / This place for what it was'; this is an important distinction to make, because the last person to do this will be the one who can still interpret what the church - though it is at the outer limits of disintegration - means, or can derive from it something that he wants (CP, 98). This particular function, then - whatever it is – will be the one which is most durable and thus ultimately the most important. And the end of the poem pronounces this to be the churchyard, or the building's role as mausoleum, which makes the church proper 'to grow wise in, / If only that so many dead lie round' (*CP*, 98).

Yet even this perception is immaterial in relation to the spiritual power of the place itself, apart from its Christian symbolism. The poet envisions the potentially ruined church as still providing ground for superstitious people even beyond its 'last' interpreter: 'Or, after dark, will dubious women come / To make their children touch a particular stone', or perform other superstitious rites (*CP*, 97). This is the closest the poet comes to seeing nature itself as possessing some sort of inherent religious, spiritual meaning. But the tone is markedly ironic, and the susceptible seekers after cures are merely women, those who are traditionally gullible to such emotional lures. Thus 'Church Going' is unusual in figuratively merging nature with a building; yet it still shows the speaker courteously detached from the forces of nature as they suggest spiritual meaning or invite an emotional response.

Larkin marks this division between himself and nature still further in his later poetry, especially in *High Windows*, though it is certainly not a conflict susceptible of simple division. In part, as Larkin himself ages and tends to write more about this process, nature often comes to represent the youth and romanticism which he feels he is fast losing, as in poems such as 'Sad Steps' and '*Vers de Société*'. In poems from this volume which do not describe nature in a realistic tradition, such as 'High Windows' and 'Money', the act of seeing outside through a window becomes a way of expressing feelings which are intangible. The resolutions of these poems suggest that connecting with nature in itself is not so important as is the ability to see beyond one's immediate experience.

This process of viewing can also delineate the space inside a room, marking it as protective. In '*Vers de Société*', the attraction of solitude is crucially tied to the poet's sense of nature outside, just beyond the confining circle of his room. He creates a romantic scene of aloneness, describing the time spent in solitude as being

> repaid
> Under a lamp, hearing the noise of wind,
> And looking out to see the moon thinned
> To an air-sharpened blade.
>
> (*CP*, 181)

These are typical Larkin images of nature – earlier on in the poem he even uses the familiar picture of trees which are 'darkly swayed' (*CP*, 181). Thus he romanticises solitude by giving it a consoling and satisfying relationship with nature. He becomes a kind of modern-day hermit; but the overwhelming impression of society's judgement remains to haunt him. The figure of the hermit is an outdated one, whom no one else gives credence to. Society's mandate, '*Virtue is social*', is irksome, though its practical manifestation of required attendance at the Warlock-Williams' party is clearly to be avoided (*CP*, 181). Alone in his room, the poet is separate from nature, from other people, and from (an allegedly non-existent) God. At the same time, however, he does not entirely want to be isolated. His inner meditation on the subject opens with the comment 'Funny how hard it is to be alone' (*CP*, 181). The poet largely dramatises an inner struggle with himself and his own conflicting desires rather than casting the conflict as a disagreement with other people outside.

The crux of the debate is a question of duty. Solitary retreat as a hermit offers one kind of connection with spiritual meaning; being in company is another, at least according to what others would have him believe. It fulfils the mandate of social '[niceness]', and 'Doing it back somehow' (*CP*, 181). Yet this too becomes a false ritual or routine, 'Playing at goodness, like going to church?' (*CP*, 181). As a man without faith, the poet can do neither with full conviction. Thus '*Vers de Société*' is not exclusively a poem about society and whether to be with people or not – it is also a romantic fantasy of becoming a modern-day atheist hermit. The hermit's cave is transformed into a room with a chair and reading-lamp and gas-fire, and it suggests some sort of comforting communion with nature: hearing the 'gas-fire [breathe]', sensing the trees 'darkly swayed' (*CP*, 181). Yet part of the problem is that other people's opinions cannot, in the end, be ignored. If no one now 'Believes the hermit with his gown and dish / Talking to God (who's gone too)', then the poet cannot convincingly pose as a hermit (*CP*, 181). Most telling in the way of obstacles is the fact that the self-examination which such privacy calls for reveals uncomfortable truths: 'Beyond the light stand failure and remorse' (*CP*, 182). Filling one's time with 'forks and faces' thus provides not only escape from this consciousness of nature (and of self) but a penance for one's failure (*CP*, 181).

'Sad Steps' further explores the ambivalence which Larkin feels towards nature, particularly as an ageing man to whom nature appears to represent a romantic impulse. The moon here possesses mesmerising poetic power. The poet perceives it as:

> High and preposterous and separate –
> Lozenge of love! Medallion of art!
> O wolves of memory! Immensements!
>
> (*CP*, 169)

But he negates this vision immediately by saying 'No', and adding that he 'shivers slightly, looking up there' (*CP*, 169). He sees the moon as representative of youth and vigour. It symbolises something definite – clear desires and high aims; but it primarily recalls the poet's vast sense of loss.

Separation from nature occurs in much of Larkin's work, and he may have created poetry out of his lack of a satisying connection with it. Several of his poems have, in fact, to do with not being one with his environment.

> No, I have never found
> The place where I could say
> *This is my proper ground,*
> *Here I shall stay;*
>
> (*CP*, 99)

writes the poet in 'Places, Loved ones'. His protagonists affirm and occasionally emphasise their distinct separation from nature and from others; even when he is outside in it, the speaker in 'Spring' describes himself as 'an indigestible sterility' in the midst of the pastoral scene through which he wanders (*CP*, 39). 'Toads Revisited' reaffirms the poet's sense of discomfort with nature: 'Walking around in the park / Should feel better than work' – yet it does not 'suit' him (*CP*, 147). The fact that he says that it *should* be superior to inside office work hints at a wry romanticism; he is uncomfortable with his discomfort. Yet he also hints at the inability of nature to be invigorating or consoling; a 'bed of lobelias' in the park only serves to provide a stage for recalling one's failures (*CP*, 147).

Larkin's remark 'Deprivation is for me what daffodils were for Wordsworth' suggests something elaborately ironic and detached about his feeling for nature as he writes about it in his poetry (*RW*, 47). His love for the countryside and his frequent bicycle trips in and around Hull as a young man are well known, and suggest an enthusiasm for the outdoors. Still, in terms of his poetry and what he wrote about his relationship to the outside world, he seems pointedly at variance with the romantic poets' embracing of nature. Possibly he experiences a sense of deprivation because he cannot share Wordsworth's profound faith in nature, affinity with nature, or ability to find meaning *in* nature. Wordsworth was inspired and elevated by daffodils, Larkin was not. Conversely, 'deprivation' (or his sense of it) was stimulating to him, and he was inventive with it. He used this sense of irony and detachment – possibly even of unfulfilled romantic longing – to good purpose. At the least, he remains acutely conscious of nature. Even though Larkin's settings are modern, urban, and usually inside, he is constantly drawn to thinking about outside and its restlessness and movement. And it seems somehow important for him to sustain a kind of communing with self in relation to outside, as in *'Vers de Société'*, where time is 'repaid / Under a lamp', listening and being attuned to the wind and moon outside (*CP*, 181).

From one point of view, what Larkin seems to resent in nature is its relation to emotion. This is emphatically true when nature images are described in connection with childhood. Whereas Wordsworth closely binds the two together as a partnership heralding glory and ecstasy, Larkin flatly rejects this notion. As his numerous depictions of enclosure in a room suggest, being inside a room represents a fundamental kind of separation from nature, and the impossibility of transcendence, union, or merging with it.

Furthermore, Larkin suggests that such union has never actually been possible – not even in childhood, nor in a childhood which theoretically included communion with nature. In particular, 'I Remember, I Remember' is a denunciation of the entire subject of drawing sustenance from nature, as well as a parody of the sentimental romantic view which holds that childhood finds one closer to heaven. The poem of this title by Thomas Hood expresses the poet's immense regret for his childhood house and garden – and for the joy and lightness of spirit which he experienced then, in direct contrast to the heavy cares of his adult life. He recalls the perfect regulation of the sun, the flowers in the garden, his swing, and surrounding fir trees – and his response to the recreated scene amounts to a longing for the past so strong that he wishes he had died rather than grown to adulthood. Larkin's reworking of this theme satirises the romance of childhood in a series of non-existent encounters with nature. The places which either did not exist or which did not yield glorious moments include the garden ('where I did not invent / Blinding theologies of flowers and fruits, / And wasn't spoken to by an old hat'), the farm of the mythical 'splendid family' ('where I could be / "Really myself" '), and the Lawrentian bracken of sexual initiation ('where she / Lay back, and "all became a burning mist" ') (*CP*, 81–2). In part, this poem derives its comedy from a specifically romantic tradition: as clearly stated in Coleridge's 'Frost at Midnight', Coleridge and Wordsworth both fervently believed in the necessity of a childhood spent in the country and out of doors. This early communion with nature seemed absolutely essential to them, and Coleridge ardently wishes it for his 'babe', the subject of his midnight meditation. Given this tradition in English letters, Larkin might well have seen it as a fruitful idea to argue against.

Larkin is angry, though, for a slightly different reason, and not simply because he did not have the idyllic childhood which Coleridge wished for all mankind. If ' "Nothing, like something, happens anywhere" ', then Coventry is merely incidental and not specially to blame for the crushing disappointment of childhood (*CP*, 82). Yet at the same time, it is possible that nothing really does happen anywhere. Oddly enough, what resonates loudly in 'I Remember, I Remember' is the humiliation of the various non-encounters with or in nature. These all have to do with emotional experiences which the poet misses. The old hat, the family and the adolescent girl fail him by not existing in his childhood world; yet his fury seems to be directed both at the vulgarity of such episodes *and* at himself for lusting after them. He desires and devalues them at the same time. On the whole, unlike Wordsworth, Larkin seems rather alarmed at the thought of delving into his childhood and its attendant emotional vulnerability. Larkin's work is typified throughout by this wry self-consciousness, and by his conception of himself as a detached observer with an adult and reasonable point of view. He is naturally moved by the subject of ageing, but in a different way from Wordsworth. He reworked the theme of the split in self which occurs between early childhood and the remainder of life when the glory of innocent vision has faded. Larkin sees this split as occurring between adolescence or the twenties and late middle age; and contemplating it was invariably anguishing rather than consoling, as in 'High Windows' and 'Sad Steps'. If Wordsworth's poetic impulse is to present emotion recollected in tranquillity, Larkin's is to show how much he despises and fears excessive emotion in any guise, often by ridiculing it from an adult perspective. Larkin's speaker in 'I Remember, I Remember' is not clam in recalling his childhood. ' "You look as if you wished the place in Hell" ', his companion observes, and the poet's conclusion is neither tranquil nor happily resolved (*CP*, 82).

In fact, many of Larkin's nature images have to do with emotion which is being expressed in vulgar or problematic ways. In 'The Trees', for instance, the emerging leaves on the trees in spring express melancholy as well as joy:

> The trees are coming into leaf
> Like something almost being said;
> The recent buds relax and spread,
> Their greenness is a kind of grief.
> (*CP*, 166)

The foliation of the trees is connected directly with expression of some kind – 'Like something almost being said' – and this is described in images suggesting decay and randomness and loss rather than purpose or vigour (*CP*, 166). The buds 'relax and spread'. Similarly, death itself, as described in 'Continuing to Live', becomes a green kind of grief, as 'On that green evening when our death begins' (*CP*, 94). Passages of this kind in Larkin's work are important because they hint at a relationship between nature and the possibility of expressing emotion – and at Larkin's ambivalence towards the latter.

The poem 'Faith Healing' in *The Whitsun Weddings* in many ways seems to sum up Larkin's reservations about experiencing and expressing emotion. It parodies the sense of merging and connectedness which some people seem to achieve through religion; and significantly, this experience of exalted love is described through nature imagery. The poet keeps an ironic distance from the display of emotion he observes; yet at the same time that he deplores it, he suggests that he can secretly sypathise with the desire for physical and emotional healing which women in the poem feel. In the course of dramatising the appeal of the faith-healer to the women, the poem shows that the primary terms of that appeal – nature – are twisted, maimed and out of joint. In the end, that is why the attempt at healing fails; the women can easily be persuaded to 'thaw' and 'weep', like the 'rigid landscape' which they resemble (*CP*, 126). But as with the grief of buds which 'relax and spread', such a display expresses sadness and loss, with no apparent purging or renewal (*CP*, 166).

The first important point about the faith-healing service itself is that it occurs in what is largely a post-Christian age. Larkin can be seen in part as a Victorian at heart, someone who has lost his faith – a crisis that he considers was probably inevitable – yet he has lived on into the modern world with many of the sensibilities of a religious man and with the moral constraints which Christianity has imposed. To recall J. R. Watson's distinction, ' Larkin's poetry celebrates the unexpressed, deeply felt longings for sacred time and sacred space.'[5] Larkin's irritation with this sense of constriction appears especially in many of his poems about relating to women, such as '*Annus Mirabilis*', in which the deliverance from outdated sexual restrictions occurs 'just too late for me' (i.e., both for 'me' to take advantage of and to value unreservedly) (*CP*, 167). A related progression of social change is satirised in 'High Windows', as well, where the poet considers that the generation before his own has been the one to overthrow religious dogma, a fact which he feels has worked to his own advantage:

> I wonder if
> Anyone looked at me, forty years back,
> And thought, *That'll be the life*;
> *No God any more, or sweating in the dark*
>
> *About hell and that, or having to hide*
> *What you think of the priest. He*
> *And his lot will all go down the long slide*
> *Like free bloody birds.*
>
> (*CP*, 165)

Larkin's protagonist often feels caught in an atheistic or agnostic position which he feels is hard-won and necessary, yet which still seems slightly unsatisfactory. The pill or diaphragm, which have resulted in the sexual revolution, seem a rather vulgar debasement of the corresponding freedom from religious *angst* for Larkin's generation, even though that is satirised as well ('*sweating in the dark / About hell and that*') (*CP*, 165). Thus the difficulty of modern man's position, as Larkin sees it, is that he cannot either fully denounce or embrace religious faith; he is left with a sense of impotent anger because an inbred residue of morality continues to haunt him and to spoil possible pleasures. Anthony Thwaite is surely right to argue against the claim that 'Church Going' is a veiled message in support of Christianity.[6] Yet at the same time, the poem shrewdly and accurately defines the multiple sides of the dilemma of redundant churches and what they represent: a religious tradition in decline. There both is and is not 'seriousness', wisdom and comfort to be derived from the empty church building (*CP*, 98). The church's main function as a place for worship is long gone, though it still has value as an historical relic.

The congregation described in 'Faith Healing', however, is still engaged in an immediate and active religious experience. There is not even a building (and thus a connection with historical tradition); the women are reconstructing some sort of meaning after religious faith has been largely discounted, and they do so in human terms. The faith healer gains power in part because he literally stands in for God. As might be expected of the character of a charlatan, the man is an American, with suggestions of Hollywood showmanship in his performance. Larkin apparently first had the inspiration to write this poem from a film which he saw on television – a fact which further explains why he remains so cool and detached from the entire scene.[7] The observer is deliberately not swayed by the atmosphere of emotional tension in the meeting, but rather coldly rejects it. The healer represents a benevolent father figure, and becomes an exalted idol whom the seekers after healing are directed towards:

> Stewards tirelessly
> Persuade them onwards to his voice and hands,
> Within whose warm spring rain of loving care
> Each dwells some twenty seconds.
>
> (CP, 126)

The nature imagery here combines powerfully with heightened emotion; the women's individual wills merge with the general movement toward the faith-healer, as they become animals who submit to herding. After they encounter the healer, they 'Sheepishly stray', or 'stay stiff, twitching and loud / With deep hoarse tears' (CP, 126). The love which they seek is also presented in terms of nature images. The healer provides each one with a 'warm spring rain of loving care' (CP, 126). The irony, of course, is that this ceremony is so perfunctory as to seem deliberately absurd; it only lasts 'some twenty seconds' (CP, 126).

Nonetheless, the initial effect of this encounter becomes so powerful as figuratively to thaw the women. Religious faith here touches a profound part of human nature, and taps a deep need. It works strongly enough to take the women out of themselves, make them lose self-consciousness and merge with their environment; they achieve that which religion – or love – ideally provides, namely a blessed union with something outside of self.

The second stanza goes on to illustrate the devastating effect this produces. In the poet's view, the resulting display becomes entirely ludicrous. This suggests Larkin's deep distrust of rousing one's emotions and of losing control of them; the effect of such relaxation of reserve is made to seem devastatingly anti-romantic. Where Wordsworth would have us welcome and even seek the child within us, Larkin parodies such a return as regression. Some of the women weep loudly,

> as if a kind of dumb
> And idiot child within them still survives
> To re-awake at kindness, thinking a voice
> At last calls them alone, that hands have come
> To lift and lighten; and such joy arrives
> Their thick tongues blort, their eyes squeeze grief, a crowd
> Of huge unheard answers jam and rejoice –
>
> (CP, 126)

This brutal depiction of vulgar, emotional self-indulgence stresses the fact that the poet considers the experience a shameful illusion. The women are mistaken in believing that 'a voice / At last calls them alone', if only because they are clearly among herds of other women filing forward to drink for twenty seconds at the 'warm spring rain of loving care' (CP, 126). Religious fervour only makes life's intrinsic sadness worse, because one realises how awful it actually is to want and not to have. The faith healer is a token figure of the yearning, which can only be speciously fulfilled. His 'voice and hands', towards which the stewards persuade the women, are not the voice and hands which have come to call them individually and to lighten loads (CP, 126).

Furthermore, though this is an obvious point, all the people who become so emotional in this scene are women. This clearly suggests an attitude of contempt for women on the part of the poet, and also a deeply rooted fear of them. He despises them all the more for giving in to their emotions and to the illusion of love. He figuratively takes revenge on them (and possibly pities them as well) by making their joy, their moment of supreme ecstasy, into an absurdity: 'Their thick tongues blort, their eyes squeeze grief' (CP, 126). Again, he depicts them literally like sheep or animals. And in the final stanza, they become a ridiculous perversion of nature: 'Moustached in flowered frocks they shake' (CP, 126).

Most important, Larkin ends the poem with an image of the women as a frozen landscape:

> An immense slackening ache,

As when, thawing, the rigid landscape weeps,
Spreads slowly through them – that, and the voice above
Saying *Dear Child*, and all time has disproved.

(CP, 126)

This is an effective image; spring and thawing of ice are normally symbolic of hope and rebirth, but, of course, they are not here – a fact which reinforces Larkin's conviction that religious ecstasy must be false and therefore must lead to disillusionment. What Larkin seems to stress here is the absence of God and the futility of awakening the 'child within' to search for this figure. The voice of God, which should be approving their dependence by welcoming and loving them, has been 'disproved'. The '*Dear child*' is only an 'idiot child' after all (*CP*, 126).[8]

Perhaps the greatest sense of wrongness here has to do with the unwarranted stirring of emotion, which leads only to a devastating recognition of loss. Merely to open the way for emotion leads to disaster: 'By now, all's wrong' (*CP*, 126).

Part of the problem inherent in religion, as Larkin portrays it, is that it does not have any power to unite anyone to something greater than him or herself. Mystical communion for the most part does not seem possible, and viewing an old Anglican church leaves one mildly impressed, but still wondering exactly 'what to look for', as in 'Church Going' (*CP*, 97). The subject of religion itself evokes from Larkin a thoughtful yet half playful response, as in 'Water', where the poet gravely considers an invitation to create a religion from scratch:

> If I were called in
> To construct a religion
> I should make use of water.
>
> (CP, 93)

In the religion which he would construct, a prominent role would be given to the images of baptism and rebirth: 'Going to church / Would entail a fording / To dry, different clothes' (*CP*, 93). But these remain rather cheerful and funny images, including 'A furious devout drench' and culminating in a spare vision of clarity yet multiplicity: the 'glass of water / Where any-angled light / Would congregate endlessly' (*CP*, 93). This poem offers a deliberately detached, unemotional view of religion, and perhaps constitutes something close to Larkin's ideal in the matter. It combines a certain amount of whimsicality with grave respect, and remains unencumbered by fonts, rood-lofts, buttresses, carved choirs and other significant though largely uninterpretable religious symbols which connect the church with England, tradition, and a sense of nationalism.

In effect, the mysticism which Larkin incorporated into *The North Ship* poems by means of Yeats' influence was later subdued by his growing sense of irony. Even the early poems tend to stop short of affirming Yeats' vigorous certainty that union with something larger than self through or in nature is possible. The grim conclusion of a later poem like 'Faith Healing', and the way it is reached, carry on what Andrew Motion has called the 'less deceived' aspect of Larkin's work and does so by attacking religious or symbolist aspects of poetry through irony. Critics like Motion and Whalen are right to point to the 'dialectic' created by Larkin's split between the influences of Yeats and Hardy, or between the symbolist inheritance and the plain, distinctly 'English' line which run concurrently through Larkin's poetry.[9] Yet there is also a related side of Larkin's work which derives more directly from Wordsworth, for whom daffodils were what deprivation was to Larkin. In other words, Larkin describes a complex relationship with nature which consists of separation from it, yet romantic attraction to it. His disconnection from it shows something grim about man's state, in a Hardyesque fashion; in 'Going, Going', the final irony is the approaching destruction of the idyllic countryside altogether: 'all that remains / For us will be concrete and tyres' (*CP*, 190). Religion and nature are to some extent bound together, and Larkin cannot get close to either. The only course open to him is to lie in bed brooding, as in 'Aubade', and to contemplate the 'uncaring / Intricate rented world' outside, with its interconnections (*CP*, 209).

He does show great sensitivity to harshness against wild creatures in nature – to the suffering and terror of the dying rabbit in 'Myxomatosis' and to the hedgehog who is accidentally 'jammed up against the blades' in 'The Mower' (*CP*, 214). Many of Larkin's poems about nature are lyrical, almost reverent, such as 'Forget What Did' and 'Solar'. 'Forget What Did' sees life fundamentally in terms of cycles which underlie purely personal griefs, describing: 'Celestial recurrences, / The day the flowers come, / And when the birds go' (*CP*, 184). Nature is not only lofty, but noble. A version of the theme of nature's generosity taken up in 'Solar' ('Unclosing like a hand, / You give for ever') appears earlier in 'Thaw', from the unpublished *In the Grip of Light*, in which 'The sun his hand uncloses like a statue / Irrevocably' (*CP*, 159, 19). When nature is seen as separate from human emotion, it appears pure. When linked with man's response to it, though, problems arise. The effect of loosening in the poem 'Thaw' is similar to the rather sinister thaw which Larkin describes in 'Faith Healing'; this earlier working again links the thawing of ice with emotion and sorrow:

> For here their pouring river reigns;
> Here, busy with resurrection, sovereign waters
> Confer among the roots, causing to fall
> From patient memory forestfuls of grief.
>
> (CP, 19)

Thus Larkin does see nature in a lyrical light, and uses its imagery to describe human emotion in a way which borders on pathetic fallacy. Yet he remains detached from it; either because man cannot help but injure small, innocent animals or because to give way to participating in nature's cycles evokes 'forestfuls of grief', he does best to remain separate and reverent (CP, 19).

Throughout Larkin's work, nature is generally depicted as something that is moving and vital and outside, while his protagonists remain inside, disturbed by nature's indifference to them. 'None of this cares for us', as 'Talking in Bed' confirms (CP, 129). Still, being a hermit or a Mr Bleaney is a gloomy calling. It is almost worse to recognise the possibility of romance or passion than to be oblivious to it; the moon outside is glorious and exalted, but looking at it only engenders pain and a reminder of ageing, as in 'Sad Steps'. Yet if one does come close to the religious experience of merging with something larger than self, as happens to the women in 'Faith Healing', this experience tends to be disgusting and exhibitionist. Rejoicing and listening to 'unheard answers' leads to excessive emotional outbursts, which are deplorable to witness (CP, 126). So nature cannot compensate for the inherent lack in religion; the two can tentatively merge, as in 'Church Going', but this union provides little in the way of consolation, since the poet must remain sceptical of faith.

Perhaps in addition to the oft-cited split in Larkin's work between a symbolist and a 'less deceived' or plain-spoken side, there is a related kind of contrast in his work: that between sentimentality and irony. He writes with all the poignancy of a man who secretly wishes that goodness and love might exist, even while he is quite convinced that they do not. The change in Larkin's poetry that occurred when Hardy rather than Yeats became his dominant influence is indeed significant; and it might in part have occurred because his native scepticism and caution asserted themselves against the broader context of romanticism. Possibly Larkin decided that Yeats was deluded, and that one cannot escape being separate from nature. Likewise, the 'Intimations of Immortality', of which Wordsworth could catch glimpses, eluded Larkin. At the same time, he began to write in the humbler 'English line' of Wordsworth and Hardy because through this style he could express more accurately what he felt. When under the influence of Yeats' grand rhetoric, Larkin had to jack himself up to an exalted pitch which was false to his perception of life. The example of Hardy showed him he no longer had to do this. Thus when he wrote about symbolist subjects (religion, nature, spirituality) he did so in plain diction, as did Wordsworth.

Throughout Larkin's work, there is evidence of a longing for Yeats to have been right, that union with the Infinite was possible. But the closest which Larkin comes to this vision is neither through nature, nor through hearing the 'gas-fire [breathe]' in hermit-like seclusion, nor through contemplating a church building (CP, 181). He records it in a poem about jazz, entitled 'For Sidney Bechet', where the sound of the saxophone becomes at last a call which evokes whole-hearted response:

> On me your voice falls as they say love should,
> Like an enormous yes. My Crescent City
> Is where your speech alone is understood,
>
> And greeted as the natural noise of good,
> Scattering long-haired grief and scored pity.
>
> (CP, 83)

3

Preserving and Celebrating England

The 'enormous yes' which stirs the poet in 'For Sidney Bechet' suggests that jazz is one of the few spheres in which emotion is permissible without being crushed by Larkin's formidable irony (*CP*, 83). Yet several of his descriptive poems, particularly the ones which have to do with seeing the English countryside and community rituals, show acceptance of contentment and a recognition of the significance of the fleeting moment. Because of his acute sensitivity to English scenes, Larkin has come to be seen in the role of 'Unofficial Laureate', a title which seems in many ways to define him as a poet.[1] As Robert Crawford points out, we have come to expect to see him in this light; there is a well-known photograph of Larkin sitting next to a roadside sign bearing the word 'England' and the pose seems exactly to typify him.[2] The fact that he refused the honour of actually becoming Poet Laureate serves to stress the distinction of this title further; if one already holds the post in an 'unofficial' capacity, the official honour itself would be gratuitous.[3] The post of Laureate encompasses both the role of writing about England itself – celebrating and preserving its memory – and being read and admired by its people. Both of these Larkin achieved, although in a characteristically roundabout way. He received notice for his poetry much later than he had hoped to do so; and for a different kind of poetry than that with which he began. From dark, brooding romantic verse, he gradually broadened his writing to include more pastoral, descriptive poetry.

What remains curious then, is that the writer of the early poems seems very far removed from the 'Unofficial Laureate' he was to become. *The Whitsun Weddings* first contains poems which later became a touchstone for this view of Larkin as spokesman for England, including pieces such as 'Here', 'The Whitsun Weddings', 'Afternoons' and 'An Arundel Tomb'. *High Windows* carries this luminous vision still further, including 'To the Sea', 'Friday Night in the Royal Station Hotel', 'Livings', and 'Show Saturday'. These poems conjure a vivid picture of the essential England of Larkin's age. Yet at the same time, his transition into a public spokesman also incorporates his earlier strengths, since he continues to maintain a characteristic distance from the objects of his regard. And the subject of a particular poem can be as much his own relationship to the vignette of a seaside scene or agricultural show – viewed from a detached perspective – as it is the scene itself. In effect, he continues to write in a romantic vein where a tender sense of loss and melancholy infuses his view of England because he incorporates his own distance from it into each poem.

Writing of an England that is vanishing, Larkin often seems like the characters in 'The Whitsun Weddings', who stand 'As if out on the end of an event / Waving goodbye / To something that survived it', and this in itself is an extremely romantic stance (*CP*, 115). His poems often seek to preserve England in its very act of vanishing, a process which makes it all the more necessary that the nation's character should be captured before it disappears. At the same time, Larkin's depiction of England is often more an imaginative recreation than a minutely detailed and realistic description. The England which he sees about him is not exactly the same as the one which he envisions; in some uncanny sense, it does not exist except as a remote ideal.

Although later poems such as 'Going, Going' assume that England is about to become a dystopia, in no other poems is England exactly a utopia; neither the Edwardian 'thousands of marriages' and tidy gardens of 1914, nor the modern-day 'acres of dismantled cars' in 'The Whitsun Weddings' nor the medieval 'scrap of history' of 'An Arundel Tomb' convey this sense (*CP*, 128, 114, 111). An essential England is an unapproachable ideal which can be perceived in the abstract from an objective distance, as in 'Going, Going', where it is described as: 'The shadows, the meadows, the lanes, / The guildhalls, the carved choirs' (*CP*, 190).

Although Larkin is often seen as a poet who celebrates England and Englishness, he generally maintains a respectful distance from the countryside and from the people who inhabit it. Many of the poems which celebrate the rituals of English life, such as 'To the Sea' and 'Show Saturday', also mark the poet's considered distance from those who take part in such annual rites, though it is an enriching rather than an alienating kind of separation – one which allows him to see these scenes the more profoundly. As with the isolation which often encloses Larkin's speakers inside, away from nature, a sense of movement and disintegration also characterises many of these poems, all of which depict England as steadily disappearing, and thus in need of being seen clearly in the present. By the time the poet arrives – or the next generation, or the 'last' person who comes to seek the place's meaning – it will be 'England gone', as 'Going, Going' describes it, in great imaginative detail (*CP*, 98, 190). The loss of a figurative Eden sustained by individual people is not Larkin's primary concern, but he does grieve for its passing; somewhat comically, the trees which are soon to be destroyed in 'Going, Going' would only be climbed by 'village louts', an affectionate term as well as a slightly satiric one (*CP*, 189). In some fundamental sense, then, life as it is bound up with the nation's identity seems to be slipping away. Many of Larkin's poems thus become elegies for England which range from regret and tenderness to anger and fatalism about its changing state.

Curiously, although his convictions about this perceived disintegration seem extremely strong, in his satires on the management of present-day England Larkin can appear petty rather than caustic. He does not write with finely honed irony when speaking as an outraged ratepayer, though many of these poems are amusing. In poems like 'Naturally the Foundation Will Bear Your Expenses', 'Homage to a Government' and 'Going, Going', this lack of forcefulness may hold sway simply because he expects no one to pay attention to his complaints. He assumes massive indifference on the part of the powers that be; therefore nothing can be done to change things. 'Naturally' the foundation will bear the academic's travelling expenses; this is just the sort of man who gets grants – he has the proper 'contacts' (*CP*, 134). As for bringing the soldiers home from abroad, of course nothing can be done if no one can even be forced to take responsibility for the situation: 'It's hard to say who wanted it to happen, / But now it's been decided nobody minds', as 'Homage to a Government' states *CP*, 171). Similarly, though 'Going, Going' posits that 'Most things are never meant', the pollution of England will surely 'happen' anyway (*CP*, 190). These poems tend bluntly to admit defeat on the part of the speaker. In light of this conviction, it seems entirely appropriate that Larkin should have turned away from the poetic influence of Yeats and should rather pointedly dislike the later work of W. H. Auden; these two writers conceived of their poetry as making a vital difference in the world, even in the arena of politics. Larkin's larger sense of helplessness in the face of a hostile, indifferent outside world convinces him that the only possible way to react is with lugubrious humour which attacks the enemy with spite. At times he deliberately overstates his political views in a kind of parody, as when he said in an interview, 'Oh, I adore Mrs. Thatcher', (something which he also meant, of course) or when he wrote to Barbara Pym: 'I feel deeply humiliated at living in a country that spends more on education than defence' (*RW*, 52).[4] Further, he continued, quoting in this letter from his own couplet on the subject, who will defend us in case of invasion: 'Colonel Sloman's Essex Rifles? The Light Horse of L.S.E.?' (*CP*, 172). Making light of these problems is one way of dealing with them; yet one senses the underlying frustration of many of these poems which seem to reflect his personal conviction that the world is hostile.

The irritated tone of these satires stems in part from a mild distaste for the people who live in England, and with whom Larkin shares the island. This stems from no particular animosity towards his fellow countrymen; a larger misanthropy is in evidence here, as the private impulse to hermitage in '*Vers de Société*' extends to a larger, national scale. He shows affection for others as well, particularly those whom he observes while they pursue their ordinary daily lives; they appear half-comically typed as 'mugfaced middleaged wives' or 'car-tuning curt-haired sons' in poems like 'Show Saturday' (*CP*, 200). For the most part, though, the poet remains an outsider and an observer of others and their rituals, rather than becoming part of the crowd with them. On a larger scale as well as a small one, he prefers solitude. Part of this desire reflects a willed separation from other people and other places; Larkin has a distinctly ambivalent, distrustful attitude to travel, to that which is not home, and to 'abroad', especially if these mean contact with a number of people. Even London inspired dislike, as he wrote to Pym: 'I do hope you are surviving in horrible London. It does *not* attract me, but no doubt it has a lot of compensations, if one can stand sharing them with 10 m. [sic] others. Not that Hull is any better!'[5]

Given this preference for detachment, most of his poems about English scenes describe not only the scene or place itself but his separation from it and his process of observing it as well. 'Places, Loved Ones' capsulises this distance from any sort of attachment, stating baldly, 'No, I have never found / The place where I could say / *This is my proper ground*'; and this elusive '*proper ground*' continues to withhold itself throughout Larkin's work, in poems about places and journeys to or beyond them (*CP*, 99). He seems to create instead a refuge of routine (work and its demands) and of self-protective solitude. Still, he is by no means indifferent to the appeal of possible escape from the confinement which this entails. Many of his poems exalt the romance of travel and the glory of transcending one's daily life. 'Poetry of Departures', for instance, satirises the appeal of this wanderlust by showing its attraction to the poet, longing for immediacy and action, as he proclaims:

> But I'd go today,
>
> Yes, swagger the nut-strewn roads,
> Crouch in the fo'c'sle
> Stubbly with goodness, if
> It weren't so artificial
>
> (CP, 85)

This vision of the adventurous life is, of course, resisted because the pull of the 'good books, the good bed' and the advantages of having a razor prove stronger (CP, 85). But its language is stirring nonetheless, and reinforces the detachment which characterises Larkin's poems, either in relation to actual prosaic scenes or to imagined, exciting ones in the hold of a pirate ship.

When Larkin writes about four cities with which he was closely associated, having lived in them, he does so with detachment; it is as though he were rejecting any idea of rootedness. In poems about Coventry, Oxford, Belfast and Hull, he described these towns in ways which either move steadily past them or which otherwise dramatise his isolation from them. He does not appropriate them as places which have meaning for him personally; on the contrary, he rejects his birthplace, Coventry, as 'the town that had been "mine"' but which he would choose to forget (CP, 81). In 'Dockery and Son' he feels pointedly excluded from Oxford – the door of his old room is 'Locked', and he catches his train 'ignored' (CP, 152). 'The Importance of Elsewhere', which again addresses strangeness in a place, describes his living in Belfast, where he assumed a library post for a short time, and serves to stress his relative separation from both Ireland and England, or home and 'elsewhere'. Similarly, 'Here' does not seem to imply that the poet had a personal relationship with Hull, where he lived for some thirty years, in any particular sense.

This scrupulous detachment from a place also tends to characterise Larkin's descriptive poems. 'Here' and 'The Whitsun Weddings' suggest a romantic excitement of a kind related to that

which he describes in 'Poetry of Departures'; to travel can in itself
be a keen pleasure. Both of these pieces address the process of
travelling and the exhilarating effect of movement. 'Here' opens,
for instance, with the word 'Swerving', which is then repeated
twice in the first stanza: 'Swerving east ... / ... swerving through
fields ... / ... swerving to solitude ... ' (*CP*, 136). This repetition
suggests a violent wrench away from some other straight or direct
course such as the 'traffic all night north' (*CP*, 136). It is not even so
much Hull itself which attracts; in fact, the town itself represents a
'surprise' when it appears (*CP*, 136). And yet this is consistent with
the poet's goal, which is solitude and getting away *from* everywhere
else. He advances no particular reason for this 'swerving', which he
undertakes; the local inhabitants come 'down / The dead straight
miles by stealing flat-faced trolleys', while the visitor must 'swerve'
aside to reach the city (*CP*, 136). 'Here' describes the city of Hull;
but it also focuses on the process of withdrawing or 'swerving to
solitude' and of seeing the town in the context of its surrounding
fields and its 'shapes and shingle' (*CP*, 137). Larkin's words of a
cantata composed by Anthony Hedges to celebrate the opening of
the Humber Bridge, entitled 'Bridge for the Living', depicts this
aspect as a comforting, protective one; Hull is described in this piece
as 'Isolate city spread alongside water', and the surrounding villages
are integrated into the countryside, as 'Farms fold in fields' (*CP*,
203). Such solitude provides a 'harbour for the heart against distress',
a sense which infuses 'Here' as well, though in a different way (*CP*,
203).

In 'Here' the poet continues to move, rather than staying
stationary and describing a scene. He starts his description at some
distance away from the town and moves through and past it.
Somewhat ironically, Hull is not portrayed as especially attractive;
nor does it seem much like home. The city contains 'Tattoo–shops,
consulates, grim head-scarfed wives'; and other slightly odd and
inelegant images, though it also remains a pastoral scene (*CP*, 136).
Hull has been described as being 'Not a place to take lightly, one
feels' by one visitor.[6] And 'Here' in many ways exemplifies this
quality, as it appears in at least some sense to be primarily driving at
a sort of isolation or definition by means of separation. The 'Isolate
villages, where removed lives / Loneliness clarifies' seem to embody
a sort of ideal for the poet; Larkin certainly valued this aspect of the
city; when talking of Hull as a place to live he described it as: 'On
the way to nowhere, as somebody put it. It's in the middle of this
lonely country, and beyond the lonely country there's only the sea. I

like that' (*RW*, 54). Thus Hull possesses the virtues of protective and beneficial isolation, and it becomes a refuge within the larger island of England.

By contrast, Larkin often loudly denounces foreign travel as producing an unpleasant sensation of separation from others, tracing his dislike of it to two childhood holidays spent in Germany when a language barrier set him completely in isolation: 'I think this sowed the seed of my hatred of abroad – not being able to talk to anyone, or read anything' (*RW*, 47). Yet it is curious that a relatively similar feeling of strangeness to some extent also characterises a poem about a place he lived in for some thirty years – though travelling and staying home produce different kinds of isolation, as Larkin suggests in the poem 'The Importance of Elsewhere'. It is likely that he did feel separate from Hull from an intellectual point of view; one letter to Pym finds him describing student demonstrations at the University of Hull as representing ' not so much a *change* in our universities as forcible recognition that a change had taken place some time ago, when we expanded them so suicidally. The universities must now be changed to fit the kind of people we took in: exams made easier, place made like a factory, with plenty of shop-floor agitation and a real live strike.'[7] 'Here' seems in a way a slightly ironic title, since the poem is less about a place which is 'here' than it is about a landscape out there. Further, in line with the great value Larkin put upon solitude, he put the highest value upon absolute, unattainable emptiness; the poem ends by describing uninhabited places beyond the town, and the 'here' of the title actually becomes located in these deserted areas: 'Here silence stands / Like heat. Here leaves unnoticed thicken', and finally: 'Here is unfenced existence; / Facing the sun, untalkative, out of reach' (*CP*, 137). This description evokes a romantic conception of a pure, ideal existence, depicting isolated nature as being all the more desirable for being unattainable.

'The Whitsun Weddings' describes a series of places in successive vignettes, but it focuses more on the train journey itself than on these scenes or on England as a whole. In keeping with the sense of travel as adventure, the poet is attuned to the speed of the train at the various stages of the journey. When it first pulls out of the station in Hull, it does so in a way which marks the poet's having achieved escape, with 'all sense / Of being in a hurry gone' (*CP*, 114). Later in the poem, when the couples have climbed aboard and the journey is nearing its end, the train gathers speed again, in a sense of urgency: 'We hurried towards London, shuffling gouts of steam' (*CP*, 115). The poet's awareness of travelling speed focuses attention on the way the journey is perceived by him. He describes a complex relationship between the people on the platform (who see the train departing), the couples on the train (almost negligible presences), and the poet (who sees the others). The poet remains part of this movement toward London, since he is on the train observing its various stops, yet in a way he also remains distinctly separated from the emotional significance of the journey. He feels no particular kinship with his fellow travellers or with their well-wishers, but when the train hurries toward London, it is 'Free at last, / And loaded with the sum of all they saw', suggesting both a hidden significance in their perceptions and something achieved, liberated and made 'free' (*CP*, 115).

The viewers on the successive platforms primarily see and participate in the weddings rather than the train journey, and this makes their perceptions qualitatively different from the poet's. He remains detached and reserved, while the crowds are engagingly transparent in their reactions; 'as we moved, each face seemed to define / Just what it saw departing' (*CP*, 115). The general air of festivity becomes invested with larger, ritualistic significance, as the girls 'stared / At a religious wounding' and the weddings take on their traditional, benedictory role of reinforcing a sense of social community (*CP*, 115). This is further emphasised by Larkin's way of describing the crowds – which he does primarily in terms of certain social types, all of which react in predictable ways to the wedding couples. The crowds appear in exactly the same terms at each station: fathers stand 'with broad belts under their suits / And seamy foreheads'; mothers are universally 'loud and fat' while girls appear invariably dressed in 'parodies of fashion' (*CP*, 115). In discussing this aspect of the poem, Timms writes that 'The objective exactness of the description prevents [the poet's] interest from seeming superior or sentimental'; yet though it may be neither of these, Larkin's view is nonetheless rather strangely circumscribed, even reductive.[8] He engages in this kind of group type-casting in several works, where crowds are split into strict divisions and this kind of listing is a useful shorthand way of sketching a crowd. He describes a local horse show in the novel *A Girl in Winter* in exactly this way:

> A great good-humour filled the crowd, which was a local one from the surrounding villages. Every class of person wandered aimlessly about: village women, looking older than they were; knowledgeable

farmers, who knew what neighbours had left at home in their stables as well as what they had brought to show; a tramp dressed in a long overcoat fastened with a safety-pin. (*GW*, 111)

The description continues in the same manner:

there were young men with raw, red necks and closely-tailored suits, young farmers' sons who pushed through the crowd on their horses, groomed and braided for the occasion; unplaceable men who stared from the open sunshine-roofs of their cars; the fantastic older gentry, hardly to be taken seriously, in archaic tweeds. (*GW*, 111)

In this early depiction of a crowd scene, Larkin as novelist seems almost to wish to stress the unattractiveness of the people to the point of satire. He attempts to be inclusive – the description aims to take in the entire sweep ('Every class of person') – but also to censure them in some respect. The older gentry, at least, are discounted as 'hardly to be taken seriously' (*GW*, 111). This desire to expose the English as provincial is further stressed when one of the novel's characters comments on the group in pointedly dismissive terms: '"This is an English crowd", said Jane. "They're quite unique. Their lowest common multiple is very low indeed" ' (*GW*, 111).

In this relatively early example of Larkin's prose writing, as in his later poems about English crowd scenes, he tends to categorise groups by class or sex or age. This tends to impose simplistic divisions; it is almost as though he considers satirising the group, but withdraws from doing so. However, the measure of his development as a poet can be seen in 'The Whitsun Weddings', which shows affection for the groups of onlookers rather than simple contempt. Although the crowds on the platforms are grouped into various types, none is singled out individually, not even the newly married brides and grooms. And this is consistent with the meditative tone of the poem. The poet seems to be striving to excise any personal element from the scene. In fact, an earlier draft of the poem shows Larkin describing the married couples as they climb aboard the train, and speculating on their subsequent married lives together. He imagines some pairs succeeding in married life, others failing; some being favoured by fortune, others being singled out for misfortune.[9] He later shifted the emphasis of the poem and deleted this particular line of thought altogether, cancelling out these possible visions of the future. This is an important deletion because it keeps the focus of the poem entirely on the moment of present vision. In the final version of the poem, we hear one representative exclamation from a bride or groom; they 'settle hats' and reflect on the overwhelming emotion of the wedding day: '*I nearly died*', and the couples watch the landscape, 'sitting side by side' in the train (*CP*, 116). The journey itself marks the beginning of these relationships, as in the 'some fifty minutes' of the remaining trip 'A dozen marriages got under way' (*CP*, 115–16). However, the journey itself, rather than the people who participate in it, seems to be of paramount importance. The poet describes the train trip in terms of his unique perception of the event, and feels satisfaction in apprehending the 'frail / Travelling coincidence' which only he notices:

> – and none
>   · Thought of the others they would never meet
>   Or how their lives would all contain this hour.
> (*CP*, 116)

To some extent, then, the significance of the journey lies in the poet's sense of movement and impetus, and of the verve that goes with adventure and travel, rather than in its being an extension of a community ritual:

> and it was nearly done, this frail
> Travelling coincidence; and what it held
> Stood ready to be loosed with all the power
> That being changed can give. We slowed again,
> And as the tightened brakes took hold, there swelled
> A sense of falling, like an arrow-shower
> Sent out of sight, somewhere becoming rain.
> (*CP*, 116)

In this ending, the poet visualises the ideal extension of the journey, which continues past the actual arrival of the train at its appointed destination. Though arrival in London is the journey's aim, the poem primarily evokes a romanticised view of the journey, in that its impetus continues. Somewhat oddly, it is the train journey, rather than the weddings and wedding parties, which is important. Further, the balance between participation and separation, which characterise train travel, might be what Larkin enjoys; on a train, at least, he can be temporarily linked with others, without having to be part of the crowd himself, and without having actually to attend the weddings or stand on the station platforms. He also describes the English countryside from one of his favourite poetic vantage points – behind a window.

'To the Sea' also depicts a fundamental separation from others, and Larkin describes the poem in a letter to Pym as 'rather a self-parody'.[10] The poem has many other dimensions as well; yet at least one aspect of it works to show Larkin coming to terms with the scene on the shore in a purely private reckoning. He stresses his separateness from those on the shore: 'Strange to it now, I watch the cloudless scene', and continues in a voice of formality and detachment; one becomes convinced that the man who '[steps] over the low wall that divides / Road from concrete walk above the shore' must be wearing a coat and tie (CP, 173). Part of the strength of the poem lies just here, in the fact that the poet does not participate in the yearly rituals which he discerns – but he approves of and records them. He watches the scene as detached observer – though also as a deeply appreciative one, marvelling at it 'Still going on, all of it, still going on!' (CP, 173).

The poem initially seems to be a painting of a scene, a means of conjuring 'The miniature gaiety of seasides'. In the first stanza particularly vivid primary colours are used to describe the scene: 'blue water', 'red bathing caps', 'yellow sand', 'white steamer' (CP, 173). But the poem also has a personal cast, and becomes immediately tied to the speaker's instinctive response to the scene. In an almost Wordsworthian moment of reminiscence, he describes a personal recollection: 'To step over the low wall that divides / Road from concrete walk above the shore / Brings sharply back something known long before – ' (CP, 173). It is unprecedented in Larkin's work, to find him picturing himself as a child in a way which welcomes visions of the past. Characteristically, the moment of exhilaration is one of solitude and separation from others, coming from the happiness in 'being on my own', as when he 'searched the sand for Famous Cricketers' as a boy (CP, 173). This suggests a childlike faith in the wonders of the world, and it is fitting that he should have been doing in the past what he still does now – namely, looking for significance and value in the trash which litters the beach.

This solitary search also suggests that the poet experiences the same kind of joy in detachment from others that he experienced as a child. Still 'on [his] own', the poet remains happily separate from the crowd, although he is now noticing or looking for different things: 'Strange to it now, I watch the cloudless scene' (CP, 173).

What he sees in the present are manifestations of contemporary times, detected with an adult's fastidious eye – trash littering the beach, transistor radios. Yet at the same time, something of the child's fresh vision remains with him, as he perceives a fanciful picture-postcard scene, with a 'white steamer stuck in the afternoon – ' (CP, 173).

The title 'To the Sea' suggests movement towards, rather than a static relationship with, the seaside scene, and in a way this poem, like the train poems, charts an idealised journey. The seaside represents a ritual which is in some sense sacred because it is temporary and repeating ('half an annual pleasure, half a rite'), and because unselfconscious (CP, 173). Unlike the women in 'Faith Healing', who fervently expect religious ecstasy, the seaside bathers are endearingly awkward rather than solemn: 'Coming to water clumsily undressed / Yearly; teaching their children by a sort / Of clowning' (CP, 174). This description ends with that which seems to express true religion, as the holiday bathers are 'helping the old, too, as they ought' (CP, 174). Significantly, no one sees the full importance of this action as clearly as the observant poet, a fact which could tend to elevate him above his surroundings. At the same time, the element of 'self-parody' which Larkin ascribes to the poem contributes to its unpretentiousness and charm. The speaker does not comment on his distance from the holiday-makers, but seems content to enter the scene yet remain separate from it.

'Show Saturday' has many qualities in common with 'To the Sea' in this regard. The gathering is again seen by the poet as a significant ritual, one which is all the more so for its unselfconscious, recurring, seemingly impromptu quality; as the poem concludes, it is 'something they share / That breaks ancestrally each year into / Regenerate union. Let it always be there' (CP, 201). The poem thus primarily celebrates strength inherent in agrarian work, or the opportunity to display it formally in tents or wrestling rings or horse corrals. The poet is particularly conscious of the background of this festival, as that remains rooted in the ordinary, everyday private lives of the participants. When the show dismantles, its participants disperse: 'Back now to private addresses, gates and lamps / In high stone one-street villages, empty at dusk' (CP, 200). The show's 'strength' is seen as stemming from this continuity with daily life (CP, 201).

Activities such as those described in the show in 'Show Saturday' and the sea-bathing in 'To the Sea' thus assume some of the aspects of worship or religious observances because they are not deliberately trying to be emotionally affecting (as compared to the seemingly false religious service described in 'Faith Healing'). In an oblique way, then, in both these poems Larkin suggests that nature and the out of doors is the proper place for spiritual communion. People's efforts in this direction may be clumsy or even slightly ridiculous in comparison with nature itself; the handmade items at the show are 'all worthy, all well done, / But less than the honeycombs' (*CP*, 200). Yet the growing of vegetables and the training of animals exhibited at the show are largely seen as an enormous good. 'Show Saturday' celebrates agrarian, country life in a way which again seeks to point out the extraordinary in the ordinary event. The people who participate are in some sense slightly strange, as are the crowds seen from the train window in 'The Whitsun Weddings'. Typed according to age and sex, the poet describes: .

> The men with hunters, dog-breeding wool-defined women,
> Children all saddle-swank, mugfaced middleaged wives
> Glaring at jellies, husbands on leave from the garden
> Watchful as weasels, car-tuning curt-haired sons –
>
> (*CP*, 200)

Still, in their slightly bizarre descriptions, these people are all of a piece with the fantastical visions of common, ordinary vegetables, such as the 'scrubbed spaced / Extrusions of earth: blanch leeks like church candles' which are on display (*CP*, 199). The crowds are neither romanticised nor satirised. The recurring alliteration in a pattern reminiscent of Old English lyrics ('Watchful as weasels, car-tuning curt-haired sons') makes them seem timeless, like the crowds which appear in *Piers Plowman* (*CP*, 200).

As these poems suggest, Larkin's celebrations of the English nation tend to full and detailed descriptions of scenes which emphasise the supernatural or extraordinary element in the seemingly ordinary. The 'Pastoral of ships up streets' in the poem which describes the town of Hull, for instance, is a paradox, but a fitting one for a seaside town (*CP*, 136). These scenes project a kind of novelistic realism because they also contain less reputable elements present in the scenes of contemporary England – tattoo shops, 'acres of dismantled cars', rusting soup tins, and other junk which clutters the landscape (*CP*, 114). Even the people who are responsible for the despoiling of England appear briefly in 'Going, Going' in the form of the businessmen ('spectacled grins') and 'kids

[who] are screaming for more – ' (*CP*, 189). Larkin's poems also occasionally suggest the possibility of an ideal existence which does not dwell in a cluttered present, as in the poem 'Essential Beauty', where a craving for the ideal perfection promised by advertisements is gently satirised as missing the point of real life: 'the boy puking his heart out in the Gents / Just missed them' (*CP*, 144).

But above all, these poems about England celebrate rituals which the poet tends more often to observe than to participate in. What seems to catch his imagination is the act of interpretation itself; in 'Church Going' he wonders 'who / Will be the last, the very last, to seek / This place for what it was' (*CP*, 98). And in 'The Whitsun Weddings', 'To the Sea' and 'Show Saturday' Larkin himself becomes the discerning man who can see at least some remaining events or annual rites which help to fill the role which the church traditionally filled – that of uniting the ordinary with significance, or making our 'compulsions' become 'robed as destinies' (*CP*, 98). Andrew Motion places Larkin in a long line of 'intensely patriotic' yet 'unjingoistic' poets such as 'Wordsworth, Tennyson, Hardy, Edward Thomas, A. E. Housman and Auden', all of whom he sees as 'centrally concerned with the relationship between themselves and their towns or landscapes, and [who] habitually express a sense of communion with their surroundings in exalted or even semi-mystical terms'.[11] I would add that, in Larkin's case, this 'communion' remains as remote, solitary and formal as possible.

He further dramatises this sense of isolation in his attitude towards what is not England: that is, Abroad. This vast uncharted territory strikes terror into his heart, or so he confessed to be the case: 'I hate being abroad,' he declared in an interview. 'Generally speaking, the further one gets from home the greater the misery' (*RW*, 55). His manifest hatred of what was 'not home' took various forms. Letters and postcards written to friends while on holiday (invariably in the British Isles) bear occasional exhortations to eschew travel. A letter to Pym finds Larkin furious at his hotel; he waxes eloquent on the subject of appalling food and accommodations: 'why are single rooms so much worse than double ones? Fewer, further, frowstier? Damper, darker, dingier? Noisier, narrower, nastier?'[12] At times he claims to despair of holidays in general, which comprise a modern counterpart to medieval pilgrimages in that they are 'essentially a kind of penance for being so happy and comfortable in one's daily life'.[13]

This exaggerated fear of travel expresses obliquely Larkin's habitual sense of isolation from his surroundings; and it suggests as well that this is partly a welcome state for him. He exaggerates warnings against travel with relish in order to emphasise his comfortable seclusion at home. Numerous influences confirm his unshakable prejudice against leaving British shores. Still another letter to Pym finds Larkin writing that Kingsley Amis' novel, *One Fat Englishman*, 'takes its place among all the other books that don't make me want to visit America'.[14] He resolutely declined invitations to visit or to lecture at various universities in the States. A letter to Pym finds him suspicious of an offer to participate in a professional gathering in Washington, D.C., where he hazards that the academics involved probably 'spend time "leading discussions" and "contributing to seminars"'. Such an idea was vehemently declared to be unwelcome: 'Over my head. Over my dead body'.[15]

Whether it was a willed decision from the first or not, once he decided on this tack he had an enormous amount of fun with it. An elaborate fantasy of painless travel broadens in his remark in an interview, where he admitted 'I wouldn't mind seeing China if I could come back the same day' (*RW*, 55). Actual journeys come in for the same kind of send up; he was, in fact, persuaded to travel to Hamburg, Germany, in 1976 in order to accept the Shakespeare Prize conferred on him by the city. To refuse to attend the ceremony would have been uncourteous, and Larkin was an eminently gracious man. However, the prospect of the journey and festivities seemed to Larkin at the time to be '*VERY FAR* from all very well', as he wrote in a letter to John Betjeman.[16] The resulting trip could not be permitted to pass without a redeeming joke. In a copy of the programme for the presentation ceremony which Larkin gave to his friend Professor Garnet Rees (Professor of French at the University of Hull) and Mrs Rees, Larkin inscribed the inside cover: 'To Garnet and Dilys, from Philip "Marco Polo" Larkin'.[17]

Other people's holidays often made Larkin sense the exotic strangeness of foreign lands, as can be seen in a comment he made in a letter to Douglas Dunn regarding his holiday in France: 'I expect you to look like some Marcel Pagnol character when you return, lounging on the seafront in a beret and chewing the heads off prawns'.[18] The fantasy of 'abroad' as mysterious also called forth Larkin's habitual love of hyperbole; being taken out to eat in a Lebanese restaurant in Hull called forth comparisons of pita bread to the consistency of shoe leather.[19]

Not all of his venom is reserved for travel 'Abroad' – simply being away from home could provide cause for grumbling. Attendance at librarianship conferences in England often produced complaints about inadequate comforts; Larkin agreed vigorously with Barbara Pym about the crucial importance of a proper reading lamp next to the bed. On the occasion of a visit to All Souls, he declared: 'Oxford luxury is a myth. No shade on the guest room lamp!'[20] Even a place as well-known to him as Oxford could cause anxiety. He wrote to Pym describing a recent visit to the University as follows: 'Oxford was its usual self: heavenly for 24 hours, then I couldn't get away fast enough. It's always the same.'[21] Larkin in fact did a fair amount of travelling, despite his reputation to the contrary. He made numerous trips to Ireland and other parts of the British Isles for holidays and in order to visit family or friends. He went to Oxford for reunions at his college and to London for test matches at Lords.

Apart from the question of the dismal nature of holidays, Larkin's decision to stay in Hull for thirty years seems part of the general value he put on comfort and familiarity. As in his jokes about the miseries of travel, his subsequent prolonged stay in Hull provided him with a source of private amusement, as comments made in later interviews suggest: Larkin felt safely isolated and protected from intrusion on the 'periphery' of England: 'I love all the Americans getting on to the train at King's Cross and thinking they're going to come and bother me, and then looking at the connections and deciding they'll go to Newcastle and bother Basil Bunting instead. Makes it harder for people to get at you' (*RW*, 54). He seemed acutely sensitive to the comfort of his lodgings, changing rooms five or six times during his first few years in Hull. Even his relatively agreeable flat at Pearson Park gave occasional cause for complaint. A letter to Pym finds Larkin decrying the disturbance made by banging doors in the flat below – noise made, he hazards, by people who are either 'perpetually quarrelling' or who are possibly 'new to houses with doors'. He concludes in mock despair that he might after all be more comfortable in a bungalow: 'There must be *some* limits to the things money can't buy.'[22]

Larkin's satirisation of 'Abroad' – often masked as mockery of self – in some ways constitutes a private revenge on the horrors of the outside world. Yet it has a serious side as well, in that it defines the isolation which characterises his life. Both parts of the puzzle – Hull and 'Abroad' – are necessary to Larkin's portrayal of England. 'The Importance of Elsewhere' in particular illustrates the role of Larkin's ambivalence toward England in terms of being the Englishman abroad. The first stanza formulates the ensuing isolation as follows:

> Lonely in Ireland, since it was not home,
> Strangeness made sense. The salt rebuff of speech,
> Insisting so on difference, made me welcome:
> Once that was recognised, we were in touch.
>
> (*CP*, 104)

Though Larkin's other remarks about travel abroad tend to claim the opposite, this poem suggests that isolation from one's surroundings can work to advantage; 'Strangeness' or 'difference' make clear the need for adjustment to bridge the gap (*CP*, 104). Conversely, one assumes no such need at home. At the same time, living abroad creates a curious kind of double life, where one can 'refuse' to fit in, or forestall disappointment by simply expecting to be lonely (*CP*, 104). The last stanza hints at this by reverting to the question of 'home', of living in England:

> Living in England has no such excuse:
> These are my customs and establishments
> It would be much more serious to refuse.
> Here no elsewhere underwrites my existence.
>
> (*CP*, 104)

This poem reflects, among other things, Larkin's habitual sense of distance from his environment, whether he is at home or abroad. It also suggests that one's home defines one's identity, and the presence of this idea in his poetry explains Larkin's appeal to his readers in his role of 'Unofficial Laureate'. He speaks for private as well as for public experience, and shows the connection between England in the abstract and daily life in the concrete. In addition to celebrating quintessentially English scenes and discerning a nation's character, he also interprets England in terms of his private relationship to it. And if the relative comfort of 'customs and establishments' at home still leave him wishing for 'elsewhere', it is primarily in order to garnish and complete that which he possesses already.

4

Difficulties with Girls

Larkin's fury against women is not so much a declared state of siege
against them personally as it is an internal battle raging within
himself. In a world characterised largely by deprivation, women
come to stand for the fact that:

> Life is an immobile, locked,
> Three-handed struggle between
> Your wants, the world's for you, and (worse)
> The unbeatable slow machine
> That brings what you'll get.
>
> (*CP*, 202)

People – and life in general – seem to have disappointed Larkin
enormously. Still, deprivation often takes a uniquely feminine cast
for him. Larkin is constantly encountering difficulties in his relations
with girls – experiencing the pain of 'Love again: wanking at ten past
three', the inability to work out why things should be so impossible
(being unable to 'say why it never worked for me'), and the
frustration of trying to accommodate his own needs (*CP*, 215). As he
once wrote to Sutton in a moment of sheer exasperation, 'Fuck all
women! I am quite fed up with the whole business: sooner be half
full of beer. SEX is designed for people who like overcoming
obstacles. I don't like overcoming obstacles'.[1] Larkin's views of
women are clearly part of his larger struggle with life in terms of
encountering its 'havings-to', and feeling continually forced into
enduring that which he dislikes (*CP*, 202). As another letter to
Sutton about his own relations with women states: 'Unselfishness is
forced upon one at every turn, *I* find, and its [sic] only by cunning
and sleight of hand that one gets anything for oneself at all.'[2]

The difficulties which Larkin lays bare exist in a complicated
tangle of cause and effect; it is difficult to know whom to blame. It

may be difficult even to gauge what women are really like; as an early letter to Sutton states, written while Larkin was still up at Oxford: 'I am of the opinion that I shall never know anything about the woman I marry, *really*. What do I know of you? Nothing at all. Preserve me from interesting personalities.'[3] This remark dates from an early period in Larkin's life, before he had had time to revise his views, but to some extent it typifies the dilemma of his generation of men, who were educated apart from the 'girls' who came to seem mysterious and inaccessible. It assumes that women are 'other' and distanced. Further, compared with the excitement felt by Larkin's generation of undergraduates at Oxford when avidly reading D. H. Lawrence's novels, life beyond the University – when they actually met and courted women – may well have seemed awkward. For anyone whose ideas or expectations of women were modelled, even remotely, on Ursula and Gudrun Brangwen or Lady Chatterley, real life encounters are likely to have been a far cry from fiction. Lawrence's heroines may be *femmes fatales*, even dangerously so, or emotionally problematic (like Miriam from *Sons and Lovers*, with whom Paul Morel experiences his own difficulties); but they are usually highly charged sensually and available sexually to men. (Ironically, of course, Lawrence's ideal was not promiscuity, but fidelity to one woman; Birkin of *Women in Love* formulates this philosophy). Still, as Larkin insists in his poetry, to enjoy this kind of intense and sexual relationship might have been difficult for his generation; not only were the right kind of women hard to find, but to carry off a seduction – always supposing one could square it with one's conscience – called for a certain *savoir faire*. '*Annus Mirabilis*' hints at both these difficulties, and connects the problem directly with Lawrence. Once the prophetic message of *Lady Chatterley* was widely recognised, the poet implies, sex became possible; in addition, this is a private joke, since Larkin and his fellow undergraduates had been reading Lawrence with admiration long before the 'ban' was removed:

> Sexual intercourse began
> In nineteen sixty-three
> (Though just too late for me) –
> Between the end of the *Chatterley* ban
> And the Beatles' first LP.
> (*CP*, 167)

As the poem suggests, attaining a sense of freedom which enables one to indulge uninhibitedly in sexual intercourse requires not only a change in the social system; the difficulties here are internal as well as external to the poet, which creates a complicated situation. As Larkin wrote to Sutton some years after going down from Oxford, (and in self-mockery): 'I don't know about women and marriage. One thing I do think is that if we had known as many women as we have read books by DHL [sic] we should have a clearer idea of the situation.'[4]

Though he did consider deeply Lawrence's and Freud's discussions about unresolved sexual conflicts as they relate to one's earliest years, Larkin seems to have declined (at least in the context of his letters to Sutton) to press the issue further in order to gain insight into the problem. He records revulsion at such a possibility, but also relative unwillingness to explore its implications: 'No, if I consider my state of permanent non-attachment, my perpetual suspension, my sexual indifferences, I should put it down to Mother-complex if I were honest, I suppose. How irritating! And nasty, too!'[5] He seems to have taken no comfort from the fact that unresolved feelings about one's parents are a universally experienced affliction – except, of course, in later satiric versions of this theme such as 'This Be the Verse', where he parodies Freudian insistence on the importance of childhood in the pronouncement: 'They fuck you up, your mum and dad. / They may not mean to, but they do' (CP, 180). However, this later poem also seems to avoid both introspection and insight at the same time as it complains about his present misery.

The poem 'Love Again' comes closer to formulating a reason for his inability to avoid the pain of love, by deeming it impossible to 'say why it never worked for me' and asking 'but why put it into words?' – and yet suggesting a reason nonetheless: 'Something to do with violence / A long way back, and wrong rewards' (CP, 215). Larkin's poetry on this subject often halts in a middle ground where he points tentatively in the direction of his suffering, but does not fully explore its implications. 'Love Again' suggests a strong desire to avoid finding the source of his misery – always supposing that source were possible to find – by resisting the task of putting it 'into words'. Even so, the more cogent source of that 'usual pain' is his feeling of being victimised by the outside world, which disregards him completely and mocks his desire (CP, 215). While the poet's rival has enjoyed the woman sexually for the evening, the poet, alone in his bed, is treated as negligible: 'And me supposed to be ignorant, / Or find it funny, or not to care' (CP, 215). The frustration is all the more ironic because the woman in question is seen as devouring; the rival man may enjoy her sexually, but he becomes 'drowned in that lash-wide stare' (*CP*, 215). The bitterness of being mocked by another's success pains the poet as much as being denied pleasure (of a dubious sort) himself. Love is clearly an illness, a sickness 'like dysentery', and unable to confer pleasure (*CP*, 215).

Larkin's general sense of frustration and alienation from the outside world is evident in a cartoon entitled 'Portrait of the Author and Family, 1939', which he drew during his late adolescent years.[6] It pictures the artist's family: his father, mother and sister are facing one another and talking about various subjects; all of these figures are talking at once, and disregarding each other's conversation, yet they are still loosely connected in that they face each other while engaged in other occupations. The father is reading a newspaper, the mother is knitting, and the sister is standing facing them, gesturing with one hand. What is most striking about the cartoon is that the figure of the young artist is sitting completely outside the circle, scribbling at a desk with one hand while looking up; his face is turned toward the viewer, suffused with dark emotion, while a huge wordless exclamation point hovers over his head. This sense of enormous, inexpressible emotion characterises much of his writing, as I shall argue at length in the next chapter; and it also informs many of his views on women and family life. The difference which is often articulated in the poetry between selfishness and selflessness seems to derive from a deep conviction that one can never do anything other than react to other people. He is so much distressed by the pressure of others' expectations that he cannot act on his own impulses, and feels compelled to be polite to others rather than pursue his own desires. Thus the love-letters which the poet writes instead of writing a novel in 'At thirty-one, when some are rich' become something whose value and significance he cannot gauge except in the context of frustration:

> Why write, them, then? Are they in fact
> Just compromise,
> Amiable residue when each denies
> The other's want? Or are they not so nice,
> Stand-ins in each case simply for an act?
> Mushrooms of virtue? or, toadstools of vice?
>
> (*CP*, 70)

Women primarily represent time 'wasted', as in this poem, or stolen and appropriated entirely, as in 'Self's the Man', where 'the money he gets for wasting his life on work / She takes as her perk' (*CP*, 70, 117). The fear of becoming entirely subsumed by a woman leads to a corresponding insistence on the absolute *necessity* of selfishness in order to survive, or to sustain the barest existence.

Despite the evident anguish which much of Larkin's writing on the subject betrays, his view of relations between men and women can be quite funny, as when he enthusiastically admires men who play the adroit seducer: 'Costals is something of a dream figure', he says of the hero in a Montherlant novel, 'what every man would like to be if he had the courage (he adds up how long women keep him waiting, and drops them when the total reaches five hours)' (*RW*, 261). The corresponding view of women which this attitude suggests is one which Larkin isolates as a dichotomy of 'men this, women that', and it defines a firmly articulated division in his own work (*RW*, 261). To call Larkin a misogynist would be an overstatement – to call him a misanthropist might be closer to the mark. Yet women tend to play a role in his writing which finds him not far from misogyny; at the least, he capitalises on the energy which derives from seeing sexual politics solely from the man's point of view, and from projecting much of his frustration onto women, thus locating the source of his anger there. This view, because it is based on universal human conflicts, reflects a dilemma with which his readers (even, I think, his female readers) can readily identify – and which accounts in part for the appeal of his work. In addition, this largely negative and hostile view of women is countered by the lyrical, tender side of his poetry which sees women as inspirational and pure, as in poems such as 'Maiden Name', 'I see a girl dragged by the wrists', 'Latest Face' and 'Broadcast'.

In the scheme which Larkin adopts in most of his poetry, though, men are generally seen as victimised while women are powerful and able to hurt or control them. The habitual sense of self-consciousness which men feel in relation to women can be excruciating; to escape from man-hunting harpies requires all one's wits and energies. Larkin's male characters remain convinced that no woman, attractive or unattractive, would look twice at them without the light of matrimony in her eye, and they see themselves doomed, to their chagrin, to relationships only with women in the latter category. Along with the heroes of some of his favourite comic novelists such as Kingsley Amis and Peter de Vries, Larkin's own bachelor characters usually assume that beautiful women will pay absolutely no attention to them. Should one be so fortunate as to meet a 'bosomy English rose', as does the speaker in 'Wild Oats', one may be certain that the beauty will be 'trying' for her part, 'not to laugh' (*CP*, 143). Moreover, the only available women are either ugly (and therefore undesirable) or, ironically, devalued by their accessibility. As Larkin formulates this view in the terms of Montherlant's novels, 'Marriage is absolutely contrary to nature, both because man cannot help desiring many women and because women in any case become undesirable at twenty-six' (*RW*, 260).

This situation poses a dilemma for the middle-aged bachelor, both personally and morally. Larkin addresses the problem in his poetry in a variety of complaints against life, his own powerlessness, and women themselves as the probable cause of his suffering; and he does so directly and forthrightly. In a sense, what Larkin does is to adopt the freedom of the sexual revolution in talking about sex openly – even brashly – all the while proclaiming that he can't enjoy its fruits in actual fact. As the poems '*Annus Mirabilis*' and 'High Windows' suggest, he feels caught between two generations. This grievance is compounded by the fact that he feels personally affronted by women; and in consequence his poetry approaches the problem entirely from the man's view-point as a victim of the system, and from the related perspective where women are seen as entirely responsible for his deprivation. He reworks this unresolved conflict repeatedly, insisting that the relationship between men and women is antagonistic and that sex consists of 'obstacles' to be overcome.[7] As Jean Hartley recalls of Larkin, 'he'd say things like "Oh I wish you could get sex and pay for it monthly like you do the laundry, because it's all so difficult" '.[8]

One aspect of the inaccessibility of desirable women – and its frustrating effect on men – is in their artistic representation. Four of Larkin's poems, 'Lines on a Young Lady's Photograph Album', 'Sunny Prestatyn', 'Essential Beauty', and 'Wild Oats', depict idealised and beautiful women who are enshrined in fiction or in photographs. Their removal from the realm of present reality stresses their unavailability and thus subtly raises their value. At the same time, when these women appear in advertisements, men are invited by the photographer and others who create these glamorous images to appropriate and possess these women in fantasy, and create for themselves an unsatisfying illusion. Ironically of course the inaccessibility of the beloved can also define romance, in another context. The poem 'Latest Face' acknowledges the fleeting nature of romantic attraction and enshrines it in that moment. For fear of upsetting the balance, the poet would choose to leave it that way: 'Precious vagrant, recognise / My look, and do not turn again' (*CP*,

53). Romantic distance is in some ways the most desirable relationship one can have with a woman.

Another possible result of distance is simply that of envy. The girl pictured in 'Lines on a Young Lady's Photograph Album' stirs his jealousy; she is present with the poet when he views the photographs of her, yet in some ways remains inaccessible. Though rivalries are theoretically long past, he dislikes the competition which appears in the photographs in the form of the 'chaps' who 'loll / At ease about your earlier days' (*CP*, 71). In an almost Proustian moment of possessiveness, he becomes jealous about the times in the past when he was not present. The girl, or the 'real' girl as she existed in the past, remains inaccessible to him. In addition to arousing his jealousy of potential rivals, the photographs reflect the futility of his desire to possess her. When he contemplates the surreptitious theft of one of the pictures, he still can only grasp the image of her, not the woman herself. What staggers him is a sense of exclusion from her life: the photographs comprise 'a past that no one now can share' (*CP*, 72).

The distance from the young woman is all the more painful because she is seen to be a 'real girl in a real place' through the convincing medium of the camera (*CP*, 71). This problem of remoteness is compounded in regard to idealised women who appear on posters in the service of advertising, and who seem actively to solicit men's admiration, which they demand without giving anything substantive in return. The women in 'Essential Beauty' and 'Sunny Prestatyn' represent an exalted, infinitely distanced version of femininity. Using their sexual powers for a specific purpose, they seem to promise themselves through the medium of the product they represent; 'Essential Beauty' depicts a girl in a cigarette advertisement, while 'Sunny Prestatyn' depicts a girl who advertises a beach resort. These are at once 'real' girls, because photography reproduces them faithfully, and yet unreal – because they are artfully glamorised and because they exist only in a photograph. Thus photography becomes a kind of metaphor for not being able to communicate with or touch a woman. Further, the women are seductive in that they attempt to sell something through the suggestion of selling themselves. The potential effect these women have on the men who behold them is, therefore, frustration: the women fail to deliver on their promises, and never appear in the flesh. Moreover, the girl in the cigarette advertisement in 'Essential Beauty' is a decadent, beautiful harbinger of death:

... dying smokers sense
Walking towards them through some dappled park
As if on water that unfocused she
No match lit up, nor drag ever brought near,
Who now stands newly clear,
Smiling, and recognising, and going dark.

                                    (*CP*, 144–5)

The girl is thus cast as a *femme fatale*; death overtakes those who
smoke in an effort to conjure her into reality, and she accepts
complicity in this relationship by 'recognising' their adoration.

This description suggests a complex situation, where the smokers
and the girl in the advertisement both perpetuate an unfulfilled,
unfulfilling relationship. She requires adoration from them, and is
seductive but does not deliver on her promises (offering a cigarette
is a poor substitute for sex) and the men are unable to break from
her. Women thus induce a kind of illness of dependency – in fact,
the successor to the 'Sunny Prestatyn' poster is one which urges its
viewers to '*Fight Cancer*' (*CP*, 149). This implies that men must
struggle to free themselves from a relationship which they feel
unable to renounce, although they see it as unhealthy. The path-
ology exists on both sides, of course – the men refuse, figuratively
and literally, to give up smoking, and thus to some extent invite
death in the presence of the *femme fatale*.

The girl on the poster in 'Sunny Prestatyn' is portrayed by those
who made the poster as figuratively prostituting herself, as she
identifies herself with the holiday beach resort. From the male point
of view, she provocatively invites him to take his pleasure: '*Come to
Sunny Prestatyn* / Laughed the girl on the poster, / Kneeling up on
the sand / In tautened white satin' (*CP*, 149). The invitation is a
calculated sexual advance. The woman merges with the place itself,
seeming to sustain it and take pleasure in it; coast and hotel seem to
'expand from her thighs and / Spread breast-lifting arms' (*CP*, 149).

Interpretations of this poem tend to be problematic, as the
poster's subsequent defacing is described in such brutal language; in
light of its crudity and intensity, one wonders how much complicity
the poet shares in the act. Terry Whalen sees the poster as exhibiting
a 'source of imaginative decadence, and also as a stimulus to
common grief and disappointment'.[9] In this context, the advertise-
ment seems to promise an impossible ideal as something attainable,
and thus, on purely moral grounds it deserves to be ruined. Whalen
sees the defacing of the poster as a protest against this shoddy kind of

commercialism, a means of 'attacking such fraudulence' and restoring 'life lived according to the dominant imaginative hungers of the familiar contemporary world'. This view in the end seems to applaud the 'graffiti [which] oddly signify a critical capacity in the common man'.[10]

Yet the poet discerns a primitive sexual urge at work here as well, and enthusiastic participation in the ritual perhaps suggests less a critical capacity on the part of *'Titch Thomas'* than it does menacing lust, and the indulging of a sexual fantasy expressed in the form of sadistic violence (*CP*, 149). The defacing of the poster may attack only the poster, and not the girl herself, but it also seeks to punish and humiliate her image in pointedly sexual terms. The poet goes on to describe in detail the various assaults made on the figure, from the mutilation of her face and exaggeration of her sexuality ('Huge tits and a fissured crotch / Were scored well in') to the 'tuberous cock and balls' which she is set 'astride', and which seem to constitute dangerous weapons which will hurt her (*CP*, 149). This catalogue of violent acts evokes the anger felt by the defacers, who figuratively rape the icon – and the scene is recounted in not especially satirical terms. The attacks are sadistic, in asserting power over the woman, and grotesque – at the least, they are intended to satisfy an urge for revenge. He seems to justify violence against women by suggesting that access to the woman is something men have been unfairly deprived of; therefore, she is fair game. The viewers of the intended icon assault and deface it partly as a means of revenge for deprivation (holidays, like women, cost money) and partly as a means of taking up the covert sexual invitation. The corporate masculine response to the photographic image of the woman is violent in part because she is unattainable in the flesh, and the men resent her attempts to use sex as power. If she appears to mock them, their only defence is to use fantasies of rape and disfigurement as a weapon against her, in order to destroy her beauty and thus negate the source of their envy.

The detached observer offers this reason for the attack: 'She was too good for this life' (*CP*, 149). This points a moral of a certain sort – the beautiful woman is 'too good' in the sense that such idealisation as the poster employs removes her from being attainable, or from being held responsible for her invitation (*CP*, 149). The poet somehow puts the burden back on her, implying that she tempts men out of her own vanity and that she also comprises the source of their deprivation. As a siren, she drives men to commit bizarre and brutal acts in response; as a prostitute, according to this logic, she deserved the punishment anyway. Still, even if this conclusion were reasonable, it nonetheless seems a harsh judgment; the lust which drives men to deface a poster can also lead one to rape an actual woman, as the poem 'Deceptions' suggests. Thus a large part of Larkin's depiction of women has directly to do with violence against them, and he seems to speak powerfully both for a corporate group of men and *from* a deep subconscious level.

To show the effect the inaccessibility of a glamorous woman has on him, Larkin evokes the image of an icon photograph again in a different context in 'Wild Oats'. In another instance of strict dichotomy, he splits the image of women into the unattainable beauty and the accessible but less attractive woman, and defines male sexual desire in this light:

> About twenty years ago
> Two girls came in where I worked –
> A bosomy English rose
> And her friend in specs I could talk to.
> Faces in those days sparked
> The whole shooting-match off, and I doubt
> If ever one had like hers:
> But it was the friend I took out,
>
> (*CP*, 143)

The 'shooting-match' is a sexual and violent image which covertly hints at the man's intentions towards the two women, and he regards their appearance even in this ordinary context as almost a deliberate provocation. They seem to present him with a choice – though since he assumes that his attainment of anything he desires will be frustrated, he knows that he must of necessity forgo pleasure ('But it was the friend I took out' (*CP*, 143)).

The women themselves embody two versions of femininity, both seductive in different ways. The 'rose' is attractive to him not only because she is beautiful, but because she is exaggeratedly feminine. She is 'bosomy', possessed of a beautiful face, and is later pictured wearing 'fur gloves', which suggests a sensual, voluptuous side to her nature (*CP*, 143). In addition, she is exalted beyond his reach; such dazzling attraction combined with inaccessibility comprises the stuff of romance. The poet's half-hearted pursuit of the 'friend in specs' is counterpointed throughout by his real desire for the 'bosomy rose' (*CP*, 143). The 'friend in specs' tries to capture the man through the use of feminine wiles other than beauty, most notably that of sexual accessibility: the couple meet 'At numerous

cathedral cities / Unknown to the clergy' (CP, 143). She also shows
herself able and determined to keep him; she is skilled at forestalling
a break, as parting entails 'about five / Rehearsals' (CP, 143).
Nonetheless, the image of the bosomy rose overshadows the friend
completely, making a relationship with her impossible for the poet.
Thus the women work together to deprive him of pleasure. The end
of the poem finds him having consistently worshipped an idealised
image: 'In my wallet are still two snaps / Of bosomy rose with fur
gloves on. / Unlucky charms, perhaps' (CP, 143). Hence the
photographs which capture the ideal of beauty possess a kind of
arcane power. The glamorous woman is unattainable in person, and
yet the would-be lover remains captivated by her image. Beautiful
women in Larkin's poems all tend to be 'too good for this life', as
'Sunny Prestatyn' phrases it, and remain exalted in another sphere
(CP, 149). This is all of a piece with his picture of male sexual
fantasy, which regards women primarily in a remote, even ethereal
way: as the poet in 'The Large Cool Store' observes, the 'Modes For
Night' which belong to women show 'How separate and unearthly
love is, / Or women are, or what they do, / Or in our young unreal
wishes / Seem to be' (CP, 135).

   The dichotomy of 'men this, women that' extends also to a fine
distinction between beautiful and not beautiful women, and to
accessible and inaccessible women (RW, 261). The problem for
Larkin's bachelors is how to get what they want, or, how to obtain
women who fit both the first and third categories. This division
between different types of women appears most notably in 'Letter
to a Friend about Girls', where the poet regrets his comparatively
unsuccessful attempt to seduce attractive women, concluding: 'all
the while / I've met a different gauge of girl from yours' (CP, 122).

   This distinction between kinds of women also includes the related
issues of class consciousness, and of constructing some means of
coping with rejection and deprivation.

   Kingsley Amis has developed this theme into high art. Women in
his novels are often seen as pawns in a larger game: they become
ciphers that indicate the social position of men who possess them.
For young men struggling to find a place in a strictly defined social
system, women of a higher social class become one more instance of
forbidden fruit. Although the tone of Larkin's novel Jill is radically
different from that of Amis' Lucky Jim (1953), the two novels share a
very similar view of women; more to the point, both novels explore
the basis of academic power with close reference to the role of
women as they bear on that struggle. Though it may be reductive to

see Larkin and Amis' main characters as 'Angry Young Men', they
do suffer in similar ways and for similar reasons; James Dixon in
Lucky Jim and John Kemp in *Jill* may be part of a University, but
their background forces them to remain marginal and powerless
within that system. As one way of illustrating this frustration, their
stories are each told from a distantly male point of view, a
perspective which moreover marvels at the stupidity of women who
fall for men with more social clout and power (Christine for
Bertrand Welch, Elizabeth for Christopher Warner). Women may
be forced to use their sexual power to assert themselves because it is
the only power they have; at the same time, this struggle becomes
maddening for the men around them. Larkin and Amis both attempt
to show the cruelty to the male ego inflicted by this system.

The comic possibilities in the problem of male sexual deprivation
abound in *Lucky Jim*, whose hero deliberately tries to exclude himself
from even considering pursuing an attractive woman such as
Christine Callaghan. He assumes upon first catching sight of her at
the Welches' 'arty weekend' that such a girl is beyond his reach:

> The sight of her seemed an irresistible attack on his own habits,
> standards, and ambitions: something designed to put him in his place
> for good. The notion that women like this were never on view except
> as the property of men like Bertrand was so familiar to him that it had
> long since ceased to appear an injustice. The huge class that contained
> Margaret was destined to provide his own womenfolk.[11]

In a way which echoes Larkin's contrast between the 'bosomy
English rose' and the 'friend in specs', Amis also divides women into
two different groups: those like Christine, who are beautiful yet
remote and inaccessible (except to cunning louts like Bertrand
Welch) and those like Margaret, who are not beautiful and who
thus must try to attract men by other means (*CP*, 143). Dixon tacitly
assents to this hierarchy which primarily values beauty, judging that
twenty per cent more beauty and attractiveness in Margaret would
render her free from the need to use emotional manipulation in
order to stave off loneliness. Yet since she lacks this advantage, she
must make up for it by other means; Margaret thus becomes a
symbol of the manipulation of a man by means of feminine wiles.
Like the 'friend in specs' in 'Wild Oats', from whom parting entails
'about five ./ Rehearsals', Margaret artfully prolongs emotional
relations with Dixon indefinitely (*CP*, 143). Dixon pities Margaret
for her situation, even for her neurosis; but in the end the novel

works to divest him of responsibility for her, to raise him to a higher social level through Christine, and to provide him with a fulfilling relationship.

Larkin and Amis do not see this division along lines of class or beauty as a feminist issue; they decline to look at it from a woman's point of view at all. But this sort of distinction necessarily affects the pursuit of romance. Women are trapped by false divisions and taken in by false perceptions as well, as they tend to attach themselves to men of the wrong sort, thus proving themselves all the more in need of conversion to becoming the right 'sort' of girl (*CP*, 123). Though this is perhaps not the primary theme of Amis' novel, Larkin seems to have been sensitive to it as a dilemma. He summarises *Lucky Jim* in terms of this tension, describing the plot as follows: 'the theme – boy meets apparently nasty girl, but turns her into a nice girl by getting her away from nasty environment – is one I think has always meant a lot to Kingsley' (*RW*, 59).

Larkin's first novel, *Jill*, also makes a subtle connection between women and the class system, in dramatising the exclusion which the protagonist feels from the university community. In his first term at Oxford, John Kemp yearns to impress his roommate and friends. Since he is not of their class or background, he must invent a past which will give him common ground with them – and he does this through creating a fictional half-sister who possesses these qualities. Women throughout the novel are signs of privilege and status; they are crucial to the largely masculine university world because they show what one is. John can immediately place Christopher Warner, his roommate, by his friendly relations with Elizabeth and later on by the appearance of his mother at Oxford. If he cannot acquire a real girl, as Christopher does, he can create a fictional one, since her actual existence is less important than the status which she confers on him. The great success of this plan is revealed when he first speaks of Jill and perceives that he has made Christopher envious; by playing on his roommate's sense of competition and male rivalry, John realises that he has attained something that Christopher wants:

> John saw with gathering amazement that he had said something that made Christopher envious of him – only for this moment, perhaps, but none the less envious. There was a disturbed tone in his voice and even as John watched him, he slowly withdrew his left hand from his pocket, full of money, saying: 'I owe you a quid, don't I?' (*J*, 90).

The fact that Christopher gives him money at this point indicates his new respect for John. Initially, then, John's tactic succeeds; if he can attain a close association with a woman, he can impress others.

Thus Larkin shrewdly portrays adolescent sexual fantasies as largely fantasies of power, of being able to force other people to take notice. Yet the danger of such a game is also evident in the novel; John can impress Christopher with the figure of Jill while she exists only as an ideal under his control. When she becomes 'real' to him as Gillian, she becomes elusive. The attendant pain of unrequited love is indeed bitter, but it becomes all the more so because it has implications for John's fantasies in terms of the larger university community. Gillian's rejection of him becomes fatal to his dreams of being accepted in the college world. When he kisses her, Christopher Warner knocks him out. The moral seems to be that women like Gillian are unattainable for men like John Kemp, and this message is reinforced by the fact that he initially created Jill in order to become a part of Christopher Warner's world. The strategy sabotages itself.

Clearly, one of the reasons that women in this novel are important is because of what they can make a man do (lose his head, try to rise above his station) and because of their power to deny him that fulfilment and their power to make him feel foolish. This is not entirely a willed decision on Gillian's part, of course – it is primarily other people who interpose between John and his love for her. First, when he invites Gillian to tea, it is Elizabeth who prevents Gillian from coming and who verbally reprimands him, making it clear both that such relations are not acceptable and that John 'ought to have known' this (another snub which seeks to expose his social inferiority) (J, 161). Second, it is Christopher who punishes John for kissing Gillian. In both instances, society's agents step in to deny John access to his dream, or to punish him for having attempted to seize it by force.

In fact, the love relationship depicted in the novel is most important because of its larger context; it becomes a warning against trusting in the illusion of love. Andrew Motion observes of both Larkin's novels: 'the only truths are certainties of disappointment, and the only way of coming to terms with them is not to expect anything else. Living, the novels suggest, necessarily involves cultivating a self-protective pessimism'.[12] Renunciation is shown to be the wiser choice, given the particular system in which John Kemp is forced to live, and it has the added advantages of freeing him from responsibility in his relationship with Gillian and in relation to the outside world. He reflects on this as follows, casting renunciation of love as a freeing kind of nihilistic stasis: 'Then if there was no difference between love fulfilled and love unfulfilled, how could there be any difference between any other pair of opposites? Was he not freed, for the rest of his life, from choice?' (*J*, 196).

This early novel articulates a problem which Larkin returns to again in his later work: that of romantic disillusionment and of sexual frustration. The problems of the middle-aged bachelor absorb many of Larkin's protagonists, who feel cheated not only by a social system which urges marriage, but by a malevolent fate which burdens them with sexual needs and makes renunciation of them difficult to achieve and to bear.

In a way which perhaps even equals the passion of Montherlant, Larkin argues forcefully about the difficulty of being a man. For one thing, he points out that the problem of sexual frustration is all the more irritating because the poet did not choose it. Sexuality and its greed are thrust upon him; they are part of the limitation of being human which he did not want. In 'Ignorance', the poet chafes under a sense of being imprisoned in his body:

> Strange to be ignorant of the way things work:
> Their skill at finding what they need,
> Their sense of shape, and punctual spread of seed,
> And willingness to change . . .
>
> (*CP*, 107)

Here the Darwinian process of selection is shown to be a random, external force which he cannot control. Such 'knowledge' is instrinic to being alive: 'for our flesh / Surrounds us with its own decisions' (*CP*, 107). He is saying that one has been placed in this situation with no recourse to anything outside the system; and sexual desire is something he would rather not have to manage. In its very nature sexual desire is recurrent and for that reason never ultimately satisfying. Even willed renunciation appears unavailing in 'Dry-Point', which describes the poet's struggle against the recurrence of desire, yet which also posits inevitable anti-climax even in achieving one's desire: 'But what sad scapes we cannot turn from then: / What ashen hills! what salted, shrunken lakes!' (*CP*, 36–7).

Just as John Kemp's sexual misadventures are doomed to disaster, so, seemingly, are the endeavours of all of Larkin's other protagonists, who argue endlessly with themselves and with others about the necessity of renouncing sex. What often results from Larkin's avowed pessimism about love is a statement of two opposing view-points, one which asserts that women are best given up, and the other which suggests either that the poet pursue something else instead or that he make light of his difficulties lest he seem a fool. The basic opposition which Larkin creates is between the individual self (often allied with art, as in 'Reasons for Attendance') and marriage and domestic life.

His bachelor characters encounter what they perceive as unfair disapproval, and resent being accused of selfishness because they have not married. 'Self's the Man' in particular mounts a tortuous self-defence against this charge:

> To compare his life and mine
> Makes me feel a swine:
> Oh, no one can deny
> That Arnold is less selfish than I.
>
> But wait, not so fast:
> Is there such a contrast?
> He was out for his own ends
> Not just pleasing his friends;
> (CP, 117)

Larkin's protagonists protest against the frustration which they experience, caught between desire and social convention. In denouncing marriage, the poet creates a satirical portrait of a husband surrounded by wife and children (and potentially by a mother-in-law, further evidence of the horrible ties that bind familes together). In the speaker's view, Arnold has become the property of his family, and even the pursuit of sexual fulfilment becomes reversed; Arnold is virtually emasculated, as it is the shrill wife who symbolically demands performance of duties from the husband:

> And when he finishes supper
> Planning to have a read at the evening paper
> It's *Put a screw in this wall* –
> He has no time at all.
> (CP, 117)

The cumbersome domestic duties which the bachelor envisions smothering a married person are heaped on Armond with relish: the hapless husband appears dutifully engaged 'With the nippers to wheel round the houses / And the hall to paint in his old trousers' and so on (*CP*, 117).

The tactic here is to be literal about what marriage could do. From the poet's point of view, Arnold wanted sex and was thus forced into marriage – and the result is all too predictable: 'He married a woman to stop her getting away / Now she's there all day' (*CP*, 117). Marriage is thus seen entirely in the context of sexual drives, and it offers only another variation on the perennial theme of frustration. In keeping with the general emphasis on dichotomy, there seems to be no reasonable middle ground. The woman either '[gets] away' or is 'there all day' (*CP*, 117).

The main force of the satire, however, works against the speaker himself. What annoys him is his feeling of inferiority to Arnold as husband and father. To prove himself in the right, he must therefore overstate the problems attendant on Arnold's marriage, having internalised a burden of guilt which leaves him furious at everyone. Significantly, he does not try to argue against marriage on the grounds that it excludes other things; the poet does *not* defend himself by saying that he requires solitude for creating art, or that the individual identity which he possesses apart from marriage is more important. The question centres on his innate character and abilities, or on 'what [he] can stand / Without them sending a van – / Or I suppose I can' (*CP*, 118). In effect, the poet seems so determined to convince himself and others that he should avoid such entrapment that he pleads imminent death as an excuse for not marrying. This is reason enough to desist, yet at the same time is an overly extravagant defence. In addition, the qualification in the final phrase undercuts the argument, which betrays uncharacteristic uncertainty, whereas up to this point the poet has seemed aggressive and assured. The fact that he appears to hedge at the last minute suggests another side to the question without actually deflating the entire argument. It deflates his pomposity, but not his passionately expressed beliefs. While 'Self's the Man' dramatises the difficulties involved in working out satisfactory sexual relations for a man, it also seeks to make plain the sheer horror of marriage (a dread which is in some ways understandable). And though it may be a satirical pose, this villifies women and casts them as foreign and other.

Although he feels lucky not to be Arnold, Larkin's speaker is also aware of the loss entailed in not being a husband or father; 'Dockery and Son' speaks poignantly of the realisation of possessing 'no son, no wife, / No house or land' (*CP*, 152). 'The View', a poem written on the occasion of Larkin's fiftieth birthday, finds the poet thinking again in negatives: he is 'Unchilded and unwifed', seeing with awful clarity the 'drear' remainder of life (*CP*, 195). Thus although 'Self's the Man' emphasises the intrusion of wife and children into one's life, there is another side to it as well; their absence can seem a loss. The final conclusion to be drawn, then, is that the entire system is exasperating. Larkin's bachelor characters generally alternate between blaming themselves for their own inadequacy in the matter – in effect, for not being able to get what they want (being a Montherlant hero) and for not being able to accommodate the attendant difficulty of domestic life if one does marry (being Arnold). Caught between selfishness and love, Larkin's bachelor becomes like the 'bleeder' who 'Can't manage either view' in his poem 'Love'.[13] The system of courtship annoys him in part because it seems calculated to expose a man's weakness; the poet in 'Wild Oats', for instance, accepts all the blame for the failure of a relationship and offers a tacit admission that he is 'too selfish, withdrawn, / And easily bored to love' (*CP*, 143).

Since Larkin often insists so strongly on the dichotomy of singleness as opposite to marriage, with sexual desire wreaking havoc in the middle, he seizes on the sexual revolution of the 1960s as an illustration of what can happen when several of these earlier restrictions are lifted. While this change could theoretically create a better system for men caught in this bind, the poet remains pessimistic about his own chances of happiness and envious of others who can seize pleasure without feeling guilty. Several poems from Larkin's final volume, *High Windows*, cast the middle-aged bachelor in a setting of sexual freedom; yet when the revolution comes, it proves a further source of bitterness and frustration. This is a brilliant subject for his poetry to address, since the new system is in many ways no improvement on the old, thus providing a new subject for satire; freedom in the sense of lack of commitment does not necessarily lead to intimacy or fulfilment. But seeing it – even seeing it as an illusion – played out by others, can reinforce his personal sense of deprivation still further.

In a broad sense, Larkin sees himself as a product of, and con-sequently a captive of, his time and generation. '*Annus Mirabilis*', and 'High Windows' perceive the modern generation as having achieved freedom from entrapment because sex no longer necessarily leads to domestic responsibility entailed by the begetting of children. The kid can 'fuck' his girlfriend without the danger of begetting children thanks to the girl's (probable) pills or diaphragm

(*CP*, 165). Similarly, the entire generation described in '*Annus Mirabilis*' has entered a glorious revolution:

> Then all at once the quarrel sank:
> Everyone felt the same,
> And every life became
> A brilliant breaking of the bank,
> A quite unlosable game.
>
> (*CP*, 167)

Because of a change in the social structure and the advent of contraceptives, the middle-aged bachelor in 1963 has a much better chance of obtaining 'Sexual intercourse' with no strings attached – although, to his chagrin, he cannot partake in it (*CP*, 167). The times are now propitious, but liberation occurred 'just too late for me' (*CP*, 167).

The speaker is prevented from joining in the revolution less because of external constraints than because of internal scruples. Intellectually he perceives the advantages of free sex. Still, the protagonist has so completely internalised old-fashioned notions of moral restraint – no sex without marriage, or at least without shame – that he cannot now throw them off. He sees himself as a product of his time and generation, becoming like the man in 'Posterity', whom the contemptuous biographer characterises as 'Not out for kicks or something happening – / One of those old-type *natural* fouled-up guys' (*CP*, 170). Similarly, the poet in '*Annus Mirabilis*' admires the sexual revolution impersonally, applauding its forthrightness, though he declares himself unable to benefit from it.

At the same time, something rings slightly false in his celebration of the miraculous event. For one thing, the change fails to eradicate the link between sex and money. Sex remains a business deal, and the optimistic hope that everyone will participate in breaking the bank seems a deliberate naiveté. Secondly, the choice of a specific date, 1963, seems suspiciously reductive. It is all too simple. The poet's description of life as a 'quite unlosable game' hints at parody; the tone of the entire poem is a puzzling mixture of sincerity and irony (*CP*, 167). It acknowledges envy and loss; but the modest self-deprecation ('rather late for me') is offered too readily, and suggests that the poet is disassociating himself from something he does not care much about (*CP*, 167). He may regret not having enjoyed more sexual freedom, yet he regrets it too politely to seem entirely convincing.

Several poems in the *High Windows* are fuelled by envy; the successful figure of Horatio in 'Letter to a Friend about Girls' broadens to include an entire generation. In 'High Windows', it is 'everyone young' who is 'going down the long slide / To happiness, endlessly' (*CP*, 165). In 'Money', the poet's bank account becomes a siren ('I listen to money singing') who seems to promise pleasure, as did the girl on the poster in 'Sunny Prestatyn'. 'Money' begins:

> Quarterly, is it, money reproaches me:
>   'Why do you let me lie here wastefully?
> I am all you never had of goods and sex.
> You could get them still by writing a few cheques'.
>
>   (*CP*, 198)

This too is a deceptive temptation. The poet's bitterness is increased by his observation that other people appear to manage their resources better: they have acquired 'a second house and car and wife' (*CP*, 198). Yet again, these are not something he wants, even though he could now afford them. From his view-point, the system has not changed significantly, not least because he does not feel that he can allow himself pleasure. In addition, the notion of having to pay for pleasure still haunts him; it still takes money to buy 'goods and sex', or at least to acquire a second wife (*CP*, 198). Even in this new, relatively enlightened system, sex is something that the poet cannot enjoy in a normal way. He mocks himself for his own inadequacy ('Not out of kicks or something happening'), though he also satirises the new system as well (*CP*, 170). The *'long slide'* to happiness sounds too facile to be real (*CP*, 165). One is left finally with the haunting sense of difficulty and pain which characterises the poet's view at the end of 'Money' and 'High Windows'. All that Larkin can do in response to the siren call of money or to his overwhelming envy of the younger generation is to take up a vantage point which he has taken up before, to distance himself behind a window, through which he watches the manic dance of life. And it can only be a partial solution to his pain; from this perspective, the poet's sense of despondency predominates: 'It is intensely sad' (*CP*, 198).

Yet given the fact that Larkin is primarily expressing a corporate masculine perspective on sexual matters, there still remains the problem of the misogyny his work expresses. One might well ask what Larkin is trying to achieve in these poems. One response to redeem the poet from a charge of misogyny might be that he is satirising men with these views and thus showing that women ought to be treated less as objects and more as people in their own right. However, this does not seem to be the case, since he might just as strongly appear to want women to stop tormenting men; it remains unclear just what difficulties the men in Larkin's poetry and fiction are projecting onto women out of their own internal struggles, and what external difficulties they have to contend with. In effect, Larkin never reaches a resolution to these questions, and they continue to spin in endless reworkings of the conflict. Another possible consideration is that Larkin is making women symbolic of the lure of romantic love in order to satirise the foolishness of excessive emotion; he is notably pessimistic on this subject, and women in his poetry and fiction might suffer in their representation from bearing the burden of expressing this disappointment and bitterness. His character .Katherine Lind in *A Girl in Winter* is particularly interesting in this light, as one of her roles in the novel seems to be to illustrate the isolating effects of romantic love and the pain of unfulfilled desire. She is an outsider first of all because she is a foreigner. When she first visits England, her infatuation is naturally an isolating experience because her love for Robin, the English boy whom she comes from abroad to meet, is unrequited: 'she had fancied that love needed two people, as if it were a lake they had to dive in simultaneously. Now she found she had gone into it alone, while he remained undismayed' (*GW*, 127). Her analysis of her feelings at this juncture are a well-reasoned attempt to damp down her emotions for him completely.

> It was little use troubling. She could not pretend to herself that he felt towards her one tenth of the interest she felt in him. ... She could only hope that the burden of this new love would be taken off her before it betrayed her into actions she would regret. (*GW*, 129)

In meditating on the experience, she focuses more on the pain and burden of love itself – and the necessity for its concealment – than she does on Robin.

At the end of the novel, she seems detached from emotion altogether, and the effort of will has so well succeeded that when she meets Robin again, several years after their first encounter as adolescents, they '[fail] to connect' (*GW*, 229). The distance between them is the more marked because they have had sex together; Katherine grants him his desire and sleeps with him, but she seems to do so as if courteously complying with a request that will not, in any material sense, matter. One of the things the novel does is parody male sexual desire by making Robin seem rather a fool in persisting to try to seduce her; there is a point when Katherine has repeatedly refused his advances and reflects drily: 'Someone must have given him the idea that he fascinated women' (*GW*, 235). Robin is, in fact, fairly inept as a seducer, and either does not try to engage Katherine emotionally or is unable to do so. Love cannot occur here – at any rate not as a shared experience of simultaneously diving into a lake; sexual attraction can only result in a brief and detached meeting. What the novel suggests in this encounter between Katherine and Robin is that women do have a separate point of view, and may even despise men as selfish beings; but for both parties, the best possible relationship consists of unemotional exchange given in the currency of 'unimportant [kindnesses]' (*GW*, 243). Katherine does not particularly feel like sleeping with Robin, (though she seems to have surprisingly few or no moral reservations about it) and neither does he want to give, or receive from her, any sort of commitment (a reassuringly masculine response). He feels mildly uncomfortable about this, as he tells her:

> 'Obviously, it's the only worth-while thing, a career and getting a family, increasing and multiplying, whatever that means. But when you don't feel it – I mean, if I asked you, for instance, to marry me, you'd refuse, wouldn't you ... wouldn't you?'
> 'I suppose so'.
> 'Well, there you are, then'. (*GW*, 247)

The ideal arrangement in this scheme is *not* feeling much, and not taking a sexual relationship seriously – and not pursuing something (career and family) when 'you don't feel it' (*GW*, 247). Since she does not insist on forcing him into commitment, Katherine seems an ideal heroine (from a masculine point of view) in her response to Robin. Yet the novel attributes a curious sort of detachment to both of them.

In poems such as 'I see a girl dragged by the wrists' and 'Deceptions', Larkin shows a tenderness, even a reverence toward women. The girl in the *North Ship* poem, 'I see a girl dragged by the wrists', possesses an elusive vitality and joy which the poet envies but feels that he cannot attain: 'To be that girl! – but that's impossible' (*CP*, 279). The struggle between two people which is pictured in this poem is one of relative gaiety; the girl laughs as she is being dragged along in the snow, and she is clearly willing and enjoying the relationship of being dominated by another.

In 'Deceptions' Larkin addressed the problems of violence and sex when a rape results, and the event here is not distanced by satire but rather brought close by focusing on its victim and her agony. The poet shows compassion for the girl's suffering; yet at the same time, the poem remains problematic because the poet also shows a great deal of sympathy with the man who has attacked her, and thus he ends the poem with a marked detachment from the woman's suffering, which he begins the piece in describing. This ambivalent view-point suggests a complex psychological structure underneath, where the poet can to some extent identify with the girl's victimisation – but only partially. He seems to show tenderness to her and participation in her sorrow *because* she has been hurt. On the one hand, the poem suggests that the poet can neither imaginatively be nor understand the victimised Victorian girl, though he certainly shares some empathy with her by identifying with her pain: 'Even so distant, I can taste the grief, / Bitter and sharp with stalks, he made you gulp' (*CP*, 32). This description is also a grim kind of Freudian pun as well as a literal one, since the girl has been drugged before being violated. Yet in a way, the poet distances himself and admits that he cannot participate in that grief, though this too is a mark of respect for her: 'I would not dare / Console you if I could' (*CP*, 32). Ultimately, however, the poet dramatises the girl's agony in light of the rapist's dissatisfaction once the deed is done; the man, in his view, attains entrance only to 'fulfilment's desolate attic' by violating her (*CP*, 32). This understanding acknowledges that the rapist's sadistic violence cannot solve his desire for revenge against women, which has deeper roots. The girl has been punished as an innocent victim, and the poet expresses remorse for her ruin at the same time that he recognises some of the impulses which led to it.

One important aspect of the poem is its seeming reality, achieved through direct reference to an actual event. This is not at all the same as the adolescent fantasies such as those described in 'A Study of Reading Habits', where the poet exults in 'The women I clubbed with sex! / I broke them up like meringues' (*CP*, 131). This obviously came out of a book – or the poet's own imagination. In 'Deceptions', however, Larkin seems to insist upon our seeing the rape as a vivid, actual occurrence, by first quoting the girl's own words from Mayhew's account in his massive study, *London Labour and the London Poor*. Mayhew himself tried in his research and writing not to sentimentalise the poor or their problems; and yet Larkin almost exploits the scene by evoking the girl's words and her misery and then turning to the criminal's point of view. It appears almost frighteningly detached.[14]

Much – though not all – of the burden of difficulty here lies with several critics' readings of the poem, which tend to accept at face value the premise advanced in the poem that the rapist is somehow worse off than his victim. One result of summarising the prose content of the poem – especially given its basis in actual incident – is to make the poet and critic seem casual and heartless. A question such as 'Is it really worse for the rapist because he is less undeceived than the girl is?' seems academic and cruel on the critic's part, if this is indeed what the poet is proposing. Yet it is an assumption which generally remains unchallenged. One critic responds as follows: 'the only consolation he can offer the girl is that her suffering is "exact". She will spiritually grow by her knowledge; the "fulfilment" of the rapist is in reality not fulfilling, but disappointing, a blundering into empty confusion'.[15] Another reading suggests: 'Though the girl cannot be consoled for her various pains, she harboured no delusions as to what was happening. Because Larkin thus uses the rapist's lust as an emblem of all human desires, his sense of shared self-deception allows him to go beyond pity for the girl or indignation against the rapist'.[16] Yet this is surely a bit abstract. It is all very well to write sagely about suffering, but this poem seems less Hardyesque and fateful and immediate than it does detached almost to the point of sadism.

For one thing, this equable view of the rapist as personally 'unfulfilled' in his action ignores the sociological perspective having to do with cold cash, a connection of which Mayhew himself was keenly aware. Someone is eventually going to profit from the ruin of the girl, and from her abduction into prostitution. It also neglects to mention the aspect of domination which the violent act of the rapist clearly demonstrates. He may be spiritually unfulfilled, but he has physically brutalised her, an act which one may assume is not spiritually enlightening for her so much as it is damaging. Finally, this kind of reading ignores the extent of the girl's actual suffering – which is so great that she begs her captors to kill her – and fails to appreciate that she was deceived in large measure as well. She is sufficiently drugged during the rape as to only discover that she has 'been ruined' (her words) the next morning (*CP*, 32). In sum, I do not think that one can have it both ways: Larkin as detached poetic observer and Larkin as sympathetic to human suffering. While not ignoring the aesthetics of the poem, the callousness which it exhibits and the sadism which it in part condones ought at the least to be seen as problematic – and as a limitation in Larkin's art.

Although Larkin wrote non-satirical poems about men's relationships with women, the underlying subtext still seems to express resentment towards women. The burden of these poems seems to be the difficulty men experience in dealing with their sexual desire and in relating to women. A posthumously published but incomplete poem entitled 'The Dance' provides a fascinating example of this ambivalence, which Larkin apparently wrestled with over a long period. It describes a particular situation – a social dance – and the poet's feelings of paralysis, jealousy and longing as they occur during the course of the evening. The social outing combines three agreeable things, 'Drink, sex and jazz', which constitute a modernised version of the traditional elements of revelry, 'Wine, women and song' (*CP*, 154). Yet the abandonment to pleasure which the poet seeks through experiencing these things is not forthcoming; the dance described here primarily offers a stage for acute sexual and emotional anxiety. At the same time, this poem contains probably the most deeply considered and nearly positive view of love and desire of any of Larkin's works. It records a moment when the poet recognises that emotion might be possible, even permissible, and when he considers allowing his defences against it figuratively to 'topple' (*CP*, 157). The poem expresses genuine regret and real pain, and records an attempt to reach for the object of his desire, even as the poet regrets that attempt in the same breath, crying:

> How useless to invite
> The sickened breathlessness of being young
>
> Into my life again!
>
> (*CP*, 157)

The negative elements found in Larkin's other poetry about sexual desire are strongly present in this piece – the poet still senses violence and mockery (in the outside world and in women themselves), and he feels aggrieved, self-conscious, and at times frantic to escape. Characteristically, his first response to the prospect of the dance includes strong overtones of guilt; he looks at himself in the mirror while dressing at home and he sees 'The shame of evening trousers, evening tie', and this ambivalence resonates throughout the poem, as in his designation of the dance as the woman's 'innocent-guilty-innocent night' (*CP*, 154, 156). The very fact that he must rationalise the dance as something 'normal and allowed' suggests his uneasiness in attending it (*CP*, 154). On first arriving, for instance, he senses hostility in the parked cars and feels he must traverse an alien landscape which seems both to mock and beckon him:

> Half willing, half abandoning the will,
> I let myself by specious steps be haled
> Across the wide circumference of my scorn.
> No escape now. Large cars parked round the lawn
> Scan my approach.
>
> (*CP*, 154)

Still more menacing overtones greet him inside, in the form of threats from people or inanimate objects which seek to waylay him and prevent him from achieving his goal of pursuing the woman whom he has come to see. The dance floor 'reverberates as with alarm', the music is 'omen-laden', the parental figure in the portrait of the 'gilt-edged Founder' declines to offer 'protection', while a male rival (the 'weed from Plant Psychology') keeps on appearing to dance with the woman and to spark acute envy in the poet (*CP*, 154–6).

But the central emotional drama of the poem, apart from the threatening elements which distress him, is the poet's relationship with the woman herself. Much of his energy goes into attempting to interpret what she is communicating, as it earlier went into scanning the setting of the dance; and he fears to find her hostile as well. When they first dance together, she seems faintly antagonistic: 'Your look is challenging / And not especially friendly' (*CP*, 155). Yet this gives way to the distinct possibility of love, which the poet in turn clearly recognises – though it, like so many other things at the dance, contains the threat of potential violence:

> I feel
> The impact, open raw,
> Of a tremendous answer banging back
>
> As if I'd asked a question. In the slug
> And snarl of music, under cover of
> A few permitted movements, you suggest
> A whole consenting language, that my chest
> Quickens and tightens at, descrying love. –
>
> (*CP*, 155)

He still cannot decide whether or not to act upon this realisation, and to seize the possibility of love – and indeed, his meditation is largely directed towards questioning his own ability *to* love. He feels that he lacks the qualities which 'Moments like this demand' (*CP*, 155). He also mocks himself in these terms, as being too old to participate in emotional relationships: 'It's pathetic how / So much most people half my age have learned / Consumes me only as I watch you now' (*CP*, 156).

The extent of his anxiety is stressed by his seeming inability to manoeuvre to get what he wants. At one point he wavers:

> I ought to go,
> If going would do any good; instead,
> I let the barman tell me how it was
> Before the war
>
> (*CP*, 157)

Yet when the evening figuratively begins again, as he sits down at a table with the woman and her friends, the sinister elements of the dance have been transformed; and in dancing with her a second time he mercifully escapes notice. The two of them 'take the floor / Quite unremarked-on', and in this setting of relative security and freedom he again contemplates her invitation to love, or her 'silent beckoning' (*CP*, 157). In sum, 'The Dance' suggests that the possibility of love and intimacy exists; that it is good and much to be desired; and that the poet wishes (at least to some extent) that he possessed the qualities necessary to be able to seize it. In the end, the conflict remained largely unresolved for Larkin – the poem was unfinished, and its last word, 'understand', continues to resonate without an answer (*CP*, 158).

For the most part, the very egocentrism, anger and frustration which Larkin articulates form the heart of his argument against women throughout his work. If life is painful, he insists on howling about it and on not allowing any dilution of his pain. To say that he has always got what he wanted constitutes 'A perfectly vile and foul / Inversion of all that's been' (*CP*, 202). He exaggerates a masculine, egotistical view: his heroes exult in 'The women [they] clubbed with sex' as a means of rebelling against the deprivation which they have experienced (*CP*, 131). From one point of view, the only way to counter feminine sexual allure as power is by means of retaliation and violence. Nonetheless, these outbursts are in part a rhetorical device designed to mock and satirise what was, to Larkin and others of his generation, a real dilemma; and to some extent, he seems to have solved the problem by devoting himself to writing and insisting on its superior importance, as he suggests in 'Reasons for Attendance'. He insists here that sexual fulfilment and artistic creativity are mutually exclusive entities. In splitting the two elements into opposing sides, 'Reasons for Attendance' thus creates a dichotomy between union and individuation, between absorption in another person and devotion to the 'rough-tongued bell' of Art (*CP*, 80). Accordingly, Larkin argues with himself endlessly: 'Sex, yes, but what / Is sex?' (*CP*, 80). The problem of assigning the proper value to it – as opposed to art – preoccupies him both in a broad, social and psychological context and in an intensely personal one. He insists on division: self as artist as opposed to Arnold as husband and father. In sustaining and separating these two views, he remains suspended indefinitely in an agony of indecision.

5

Strong Language

Jazz, *Required Writing* and poetry

Larkin's scintillating anger extends far beyond the difficulties of dealing with women; his outspokenness on several points (political and artistic) has earned him the unofficial title of 'Philistine' as well as misogynist. Though these qualities in his thinking may be exaggerated by his critics, there remains a sense in which he rejoices in and capitalises on his own opinions, often expressing them in appropriately strong language. He is impassioned about the excitement of 1930s and 40s jazz, the captivating thrill of Ian Fleming's James Bond novels and in his disdain for Picasso's art – and the time and energy he devotes to these subjects make it somewhat difficult to take him seriously as an intellectual. His views on art can be broadly characterised as a mix of enthusiasms and hates. Most of all, he seems driven throughout his writing career to pursue his own views in defiance of what he senses other people want him to believe. A typical comment in his critical writings is the following statement, defending his views of John Betjeman's poetry: 'This may not be an orthodox critical judgement, but I don't see why it shouldn't be taken into account' (*RW*, 214). He seems to draw stimulation from pitting his rage against other writers' views, since he is often more determined to stress a conflicting view in opposition to someone else's ideas than he is to allow for diversity of critical view-points. The 'punch-ups' he imagines in discussions of Betjeman's reputation in Britain are a case in point (*RW*, 204). He relishes a good fight (much as Dixon in *Lucky Jim* might 'switch to simplicity' by inquiring of Bertrand Welch '"Do you know what you look like in that beard?"') and his style is often calculated to strike this tone.[1] For matters about which he feels passionately, Larkin uses strong language.

Yet it also serves a distinct purpose in his criticism, where he uses it to stress his own instinctive feelings about a work of art. As he wrote to Sutton on the occasion of hearing that *Jill* had been accepted for publication: 'The artistic process is identifying yourself more and more closely with whatever you take pleasure in, discovering its structure and significance and subtle delight. NO ARTIST SHOULD GIVE A 2d TURD FOR WHAT DOES NOT GIVE HIM PLEASURE. I 'ave spoken.'[2] Larkin's criticism as well as his art both spring from this conviction.

This forcefulness is evident in Larkin's own poetic diction as well: the presence of words like 'fucking' (used as a verb, not an adjective) and 'a load of crap' indicate a delight in a kind of anti-intellectual streak (*CP*, 165, 131). Such words would not be so shocking if they did not appear in the context of his poetry, notable for its conservatism and decorousness in style, tone and form. As Barbara Everett observes, 'Larkin's four-letter words ... may offend precisely because they figure in an idiom otherwise so well-behaved or well-adjusted, even so cautiously temperate.'[3] If such language is meant to shock us when we read it – it certainly exhilarated him to write it – it succeeds. On the other hand, though, vulgar language can seem the most conventional of protests; he draws from the flat, uninventive pool of words held in common by the prototypical 'common man'. Such language does raise the question of whether Larkin (or the speaker in a given poem) is in fact announcing his solidarity with the common man, or whether he might be cultivating an adolescent sensibility in order to shock his readers. It is also possible that Larkin, in using this diction, means exactly what he says, and that what we hear in the poetry, is neither a bitter satirist nor a distanced persona. He habitually tended to 'swear like any trooper' himself.[4] Jean Hartley observes of Larkin that he adopted vulgar language as a kind of stimulating hobby: 'He had a wonderful line in obscenity, great long well-constructed curses.'[5] Thus his poetry, prose writings and speech in private (and sometimes public) life form a continuum which suggests that vulgar language is invigorating. He wrote to Sutton, 'As a character in my book says ... "A soul and a dirty mind are practically indistinguishable."'[6] Swearing also made communication possible. As he explains to Sutton later, it is a necessary idiom for expressing the otherwise inexpressible: 'I agree about swearing. I once tried to explain to one of the borrowers here [in the library] ... [a girl at Somerville College] ... that there were certain moments in life only expressible by a flurry of filthy language.'[7]

Larkin's forcefulness as a writer goes beyond the presence of a few four-letter words. Part of his complex nature is to be passionately, blindly furious, and to strike out at the world around him. This aspect of his work often seems to rouse a strong reaction from his readers. The very force of critics' responses to Larkin's work seem in a way excessive; and yet it may be an appropriate response to the kind of sub-text lurking below the surface of Larkin's work – or, indeed, proclaiming opinions quite openly on the surface. A whole complex of bawdy, raucous, and generally 'unprintable' matter seems to underlie Larkin's *oeuvre*. There is a facet to Larkin's character which distinctly echoes Jim Dixon of Amis' *Lucky Jim*, especially in that he often seems to have such pent-up fury that it can only be released in a torrent of words or gestures – mostly directed against others, and largely expressed in private.[8] Though any direct equation of the two must be heavily qualified, one does see them as kindred spirits. 'Filthy Mozart', for instance, is said to have been Larkin's own expression, a phrase of absolute incongruity except in the context of an 'Angry Young Man' sort of protest, namely one directed against the pretension of a man like Professor Welch.[9] Both Larkin and the fictional character Jim tend to project their own fears of retaliation onto the world, and to see it as all-powerful and hostile.

Larkin enjoyed cultivating and even exaggerating this philistine, slightly violent side of his character. He pictured himself to friends as the typical man sprawled out on the couch of an evening, watching wrestling on the telly.[10] In interviews, he consistently denied literary pretensions, and went on record as never having heard of Borges. (The tone of the interviewer's question which elicits this response is mildly condescending, in fact, and almost invites such a response: 'Is Jorge Luis Borges the only other contemporary poet of note who is also a librarian, by the way? Are you aware of any others?' Larkin's reply which praises Archibald MacLeish for his superior skills *as* a librarian, suggests that such an academic distinction as 'poet librarian' is irrelevant. Larkin's question 'Who's Jorge Luis Borges?' asks as much what his claim to fame is (has *he* reorganised any libraries?) as who the man is. (*RW*, 60).) He presented himself as a humble man with simple literary tastes, reading and rereading only thrillers, detective novels, or English classics such as those by Dickens or Trollope. Larkin's reading habits can even be discussed in terms of what his reading excludes rather than what it includes: 'I read everything except philosophy, theology, economics, sociology, science, or anything to do with the wonders of nature, anything to do with technology . . . have I said politics? I'm trying to think of all the Dewey decimal classes' (*RW*, 53). What this comes down to, of course, is that Larkin claims to read virtually only novels, and to be like Dylan Thomas, who 'never read anything hard' (*RW*, 53). However, his way of expressing this is to emphasise that which he avoids, on the self-defensive assumption that no one will respect him as an intellectual anyway.

Why did Larkin *not* like reading anything 'hard'? He claims he would have been unable to understand it, remarking in an interview that he does not possess the 'kind' of mind which would digest other people's ideas; his is not, so he says, 'conceptual or ratiocinative or whatever it is' (*RW*, 60). The first-class degree which Larkin was awarded at Oxford might belie this to a great extent. He certainly did not become an academic, as he delights in pointing out, yet apart from a temperamental aversion to intellectual pursuits, I think that he avoids hard books and ideas largely because they pose too great a threat to his own ideas and creativity. While he was still up at Oxford, he wrote revealingly on the subject to Sutton, proclaiming: 'I shall never be a "scholar" or even have really much delight in the "classics.". It is becoming born upon me that literature is a very tiny thing compared with one's own life (and, of course, one's own literature). Nor shall I ever have much "taste". Life and literature is a question of what one thrills to . . .'[11] His conception of the critic's task, stated in a later interview, presupposes that this is largely a question of judging others' works . . . of '[saying] why one poem was "better" than another, and so on' (*RW*, 61). Making this kind of judgement can be death to the artistic impulse, and to his commitment to finding where pleasure lay for him.

Furthermore, if Oxford comprises 'ten thousand people all much cleverer than you are', it would be much better not to compete in an intellectual arena at all.[12] For one thing, to have his own views criticised in turn would seem insupportable; therefore he flings down a gauntlet to the academic world by saying, in effect, that he refuses even to deal with its 'hard' ideas or writing. Second, while up at Oxford himself, he seems busy trying to overthrow previous repressions and restrictions. He strove to tap his emotions, and one way to do this was to adopt D. H. Lawrence as a mentor. Lawrence also disdained academic intellectualising – and moreover, Lawrence's novels were all the more exhilarating because illicit and full of the fascinating topic of sex. They fell outside the course of canonised reading – *Lady Chatterley's Lover* ('the greatest piece of writing in the world', in Larkin's view at the time) possessed the even greater distinction of having been banned.[13] Thus in bypassing the accepted academic reading, Larkin mined a rich vein of exciting and subversive material.

This reading pattern also is part of his plan, worked out at Oxford and carried on later, of trying to create art out of his subconscious, and this endeavour stemmed from his understanding of Freud's psychoanalytic theories. Also, of course, it must be stressed that Lawrence was a cult figure for several of Larkin's fellow undergraduates; his unbounded admiration for Lawrence was shared. However, Larkin appropriated Lawrence for himself to an enormous extent by identifying him as the person whom he was most like. He felt that others' appreciation of Lawrence was, moreover, insufficient, as a comic rejoinder to one of them shows. When asked by a fellow undergraduate how one should 'approach Lawrence', Larkin (as he wrote to Sutton) suppressed the impulse to reply 'on your knees'.

To some extent, Larkin wanted so intensely to *be an artist* that this excluded for him the possibility of being an academic. Never one for half-measures, he exorcised the threat of criticism by turning to outside reading material and by elevating it to Olympic stature. Thus Lawrence became someone for a young writer to worship, or to invoke in order to receive power, while *Beowulf* and other Old English texts – lifeless in comparison with Lawrence – became objects of loathing.

Larkin may have felt ashamed of his youthful enthusiasm for Lawrence, for he scarcely mentions him after he goes down from Oxford. Hardy becomes the benign, respectable mentor of Larkin's middle years; and Hardy in his own way was a writer who was seen as distinctly unacademic, or outside the accepted system of the brokerage of intellectual ideas. In his early thirties, Larkin seems to change his vision (and his public image); the fiery, passionate young artist ('taking' one of Lawrence's letters 'as one might take an aspirin') becomes the no-nonsense man who at least knows crap when he sees it.[14] In a variant of his strategy of being the outsider at Oxford (an artist among academics) he later modified his artist persona to make himself appear a plain-speaking commoner among artists. In both cases, he defines himself as outside the pale. Thus he inflated another balloon image of himself – the poet of the common man – as a defence against *not* being sophisticated, accepted, or included in the academic inner ring. But this strategy too has a subversive twist to it, in that it caricatures culture-mongers or academics as ignorant and pretentious people. Again, to draw an illustration from *Lucky Jim*, such a situation can be wildly funny. At the Welches' 'arty weekend,' a political discussion between Dixon, Christine and Bertrand satirises this conception of artistic taste as an accepted tenet. Dixon's views are discounted by the other two entirely, and in these terms: 'Bertrand and his girl were looking at each other with identical expressions, shaking their heads, smiling, raising their eyebrows, sighing. It was as if Dixon had just said that he didn't know anything about art, but he did know what he liked.'[15] The joke, as Christine comes to see eventually, is really on them.

Larkin's adoption of the role of philistine poet was a brilliant stroke, not least because it suited him so well. Barbara Everett recalls, for instance, a joke which he made about being 'one of Nature's Orange-Men'.[16] In its own way, this transformation was particularly apt because the pose allowed him to return to his family's conservative political convictions. It also suited the neurotic view of the world which Larkin so wittily adopted, where one has to work hard to earn anything, and there is no pleasure without pain. The 'common man' role seems to have been one that he enjoyed playing exceedingly, as it provided a way of expressing his disappointment and frustration *with* this state of affairs, and gave him a new source of metaphors on which to draw. He was delighted, for instance, with the publishing success of his collection *Required Writing*, which he saw in terms of a victorious rugby match. He wrote to Douglas Dunn: 'The sales of *Required Writing* continue to amaze. I go around chalking MIDDLEBROW LITERARY CHAT RULES OK on walls.'[17] Similarly, the joint venture of a Faber cassette of Larkin and Dunn reading their poetry finds Larkin writing to his friend: 'Hope it sells, though I bet it won't. 5% of £6.95 is ... is ... .3475p, [sic] thanks very much. Shan't get fat on that.'[18]

To some extent, of course, the philistine pose was a clever projection, designed to create a self-protective image. As several critics have suspected, Larkin was probably much more widely read than he let on. Crawford points out the following discrepancies: 'In an interview he says "I'm afraid I know very little about American poetry"; a moment later he makes a joke about John Ashbery; earlier he's revealed that he's been reading Frank O'Hara. To see Larkin as some sort of simple Little Englander is as naive as seeing Burns as an English Man of Letters.'[19] Somewhat surprisingly, in light of his later antipathy to modernism, an early and quite strong influence on Larkin was Virginia Woolf.[20] Other early influences on him while he was at Oxford, in addition to Lawrence, included Isherwood, Auden, Mansfield and Dylan Thomas. All the same, he enjoyed this pose of not having literary pretensions, exaggerating the view of himself as a person of no account. The declaration that Oxford comprises a vast number of people who are 'much cleverer than you are' is perhaps intended to say as much about Oxford's conception of itself as a community as about Larkin's relationship to it.[21] Nonetheless, such exclusion (either real or imagined) seems to wound him deeply; 'Dockery and Son' casts the situation in terms of understated grief, as the visiting protagonist leaves Oxford: 'I catch my train, ignored' (*CP*, 152).

Many of Larkin's comments about art in fact suggest a pose which shows him primarily defining himself in relation to other people, in a kind of uneasy defensiveness. In an early interview, for instance, Larkin says of jazz:

> In many ways I prefer it to poetry. I listen to it while dressing in the morning, turning to it in a way I should turn to poetry if I were living my life according to Vernon Watkins's standards. What did Baudelaire say, man can live a week without bread but not a day without poetry. You might say I can live a week without poetry but not a day without jazz.[22]

This defines Larkin's view of art (preference for jazz to poetry) in relation to two figures: Watkins, whom he genuinely admires for his 'pure devotion' to poetry, and Baudelaire, whom Larkin ingenuously exposes as an aesthete, tackling him on the grounds of another sort of exaggeration. It suggests a sly kind of reversal, or an appropriation of one grandly symbolic claim for another, in justifying Larkin's own self-confessed middle-brow tastes.

Larkin's wit not only displays self-defensiveness, but suggests the sense of fun he had with his inventiveness. If he does project his own anxieties onto the world and then take up arms against it, his readers can delight in participating vicariously in that battle; and this is one reason for his appeal. A particularly vivid instance of this dramatic view of the world is the frame containing two photographs of 'Guy the Gorilla' which held prominent place in Larkin's office at the Brynmor Jones Library. These pictures of a gorilla in a zoo were apparently seen by Larkin in the newspaper while he was away from Hull on holiday. They elicited an immediate and keen response. He wrote to his secretary with imaginative interpretations of the photographs: 'In *The Telegraph* he is clearly saying "tell that bastard [X] to get stuffed!" In *The Times* his fury is wordless but huge.' The letter ends with an imperative summons: 'We *must get copies*.'[23] The gorilla becomes a kind of metaphor for Larkin's own dilemma; as his secretary later commented in a BBC interview, 'And on this table by the window he had a framed photograph of Guy the Gorilla. He admired this creature very much. I think he himself thought he was a prisoner, as Guy was.'[24]

Larkin's prose suggests at times a tantalising possibility that he feels or knows much more than he is prepared to tell, out of decency and politeness. A letter to three library employees who pretend to resign while Larkin is away on holiday evokes a playful response. Reminding the women of his continual warning that one does not come to work to be happy, he goes on to point himself as a moral: 'How long do you think I should have lasted if I had allowed myself to be influenced by the presence of Professor ——, Dr ——, and Mr ——?'[25]

In denouncing the tiresomeness of public discourse, Larkin offers occasional glimpses in his work of a zany world peopled with ogres and giants; with idiots who make life extremely tiring and whom one would like to make faces at. The most ordinary circumstances can seem menacing and hostile, as in the mock fear inspired by recent releases in a 1971 jazz review: 'Rank on rank of shiny LP covers all depicted the same thing: a bunch of young people, mostly male, with clothes and faces appropriate to criminal vagrancy, stood scowling at me in attitudes eloquent of "We're gonna do you, Dad"' (*AWJ*, 270). This attitude is characteristic of a basic impulse to see things outside in extreme terms – and as threats. And the humour is of the sort which leads to outlandish and menacing remarks like these comments about children: 'Until I grew up I thought I hated everybody, but when I grew up I realised it was just children I didn't like' (*RW*, 48). In a review of a book on children's literature, he further deplores them, citing as examples an entirely negative list of traits, including their 'noise, their nastiness, their boasting, their back-answers, their cruelty, their silliness' (*RW*, 111). As with the threatening delinquents on the LP covers, escape from their company, as from an enemy, offers blessed relief: 'The knowledge that I should never (except by deliberate act of folly) get mixed up with them again more than compensated for having to start earning a living' (*RW*, 111). Often his vision of life tends vigorously to contrast extremes of good and bad, adults and children ('vulgar little brutes' (*RW*, 111)), vintage jazz and contemporary jazz ('tending towards the silly, the disagreeable and the frigid' (*AWJ*, 112)). In consequence, Larkin employs stern and telling understatement balanced by violent exaggeration in expressing the infinite patience necessary to live in such trying circumstances. And this characteristic finds full expression in his own critical writings.

He is constantly insisting that in matters of artistic judgement one should trust one's instincts and champion popular culture (most notably jazz, but also including thrillers and light verse). In his criticism, Larkin often implies that he does not know art, but he knows what he likes – or if he does know 'Art', he would prefer to discount any mere knowledge in favour of gut reaction. His views on the subject are a curious blend of self-proclaimed Philistinism and extremely shrewd and thoughtful judgements. In an unvarying devotion to the merits of sincerity, Larkin stated repeatedly throughout his writing career that he thought artists should write directly out of their own lives, thoughts and experiences. His repeated exhortations to Sutton on this point suggest the necessity of keeping others at bay while one is creating: 'The reader doesn't come into the poem at all. . . . Poetry is nobody's business except the poet's and everybody else can fuck off.'[26]

Yet in his later formulations of this idea, the audience is seen to play a crucial role in the creative process. Larkin insisted on the importance of a kind of *laissez-faire* system of spiritual economics for the arts, whereby the audience become consumers who pay for what they like and therefore indirectly guide the artist back to a sort of native honesty about his experience, which he then shares with others through his work. More precisely, there should be an interdependent relationship between artist, poem and reader – namely that person *in* whom the poem should 're-create' the original experience or feeling which set the poet to writing. Larkin feels that 'poetry, like all art, is inextricably bound up with giving pleasure, and if a poet loses his pleasure-seeking audience he has lost the only audience worth having' (*RW*, 82–3). Though in many ways this description of the writing process makes sense, it is somewhat reductive – it is less simplistic, of course, than his earlier views in which the poet alone communes with his poem and everyone else can 'fuck off'. But it casts things in a way which shows him again cutting out a particular person in order to reach a new concensus: rather than the reader being banished, here the critic is deliberately bypassed in favour of a close connection between the poet, his work and his audience.

Larkin wrote about his own artistic aims in 1955, in a piece not intended for publication, which in part accounts for its severe tone:

I write poems to preserve things I have seen/thought/felt (if I may so indicate a composite and complex experience) both for myself and for others, though I feel my prime responsibility is to the experience itself, which I am trying to keep from oblivion for its own sake. Why I should do this I have no idea, but I think the impulse to preserve lies at the bottom of all art. (*RW*, 79)

His remains a very democratic and a reader-based view; 'First and foremost, writing poems should be a pleasure. So should reading them, by God', he stated in an interview (*RW*, 68). This seems to express a radically different view from modernism, which is primarily concerned with the work of art itself and with the artist who creates it; and with these entities as separate from other considerations of the reader's response. It is ironic that Larkin seeks to liberate himself from the tyranny of modernism by means of bashing earlier conceptions of art – in its way, a fairly modernist response.

These critical views seem to reflect another aspect of the split between Yeats and Hardy which Larkin defined near the beginning of his writing career. The relief at not having to jack oneself up to elevated emotional heights in writing poetry may well have extended to his prose as well. To some extent, this anti-cultural bent is no new revelation. Larkin had roundly denounced many of the classic English literary texts while still up at Oxford. Kingsley Amis observes: 'I have no recollection of ever hearing Philip admit to having enjoyed, or again to being ready to tolerate, any author or book he studied, with the possible exception of Shakespeare.' Significantly, Amis adds the following anecdote which describes Larkin's handwritten note on the last page of a text of a college copy of *The Faerie Queene*:

'First I thought Troilus and Criseyde was the most *boring* poem in English. Then I thought Beowulf was. Then I thought Paradise Lost was. Now I *know* that The Faerie Queene is the *dullest thing out. Blast* it.' (I queried the uncharacteristically non-alcoholic language with him; he retorted that he had not dared to aggravate his offence by writing down the words he was thinking.)[27]

At the same time, Larkin seems faintly uneasy about his relative indifference to higher art and defends himself for preferring jazz to poetry. His notion of the world as a hostile place which engenders helpless rage extends to the subject of art as well. Here the main bullies are the critics and academicians whom he designates as pompous and self-serving. In his view, the university system feeds off of modernism like a swollen parasite, explicating deliberately unclear (and possibly worthless) writing: he satirises this in the 'Introduction' to *All What Jazz* in his parody of a professorial pronouncement to potential students, regarding the subject of contemporary art: 'You've got to work at this: after all, you don't expect to understand anything as important as art straight off, do you? I mean, this is pretty complex stuff: if you want to know how complex, I'm giving a course of ninety-six lectures at the local college, starting next week, and you'd be more than welcome' (*AWJ*, 23). Clearly, he hates pretension, especially in academic dress.

Yet at the same time, it is possible that part of what he fears is criticism itself, and the crippling effect that it could have on his ability to write. There is a certain strategy in all of this which suggests that he is getting the first word in before others can criticise him; as he writes to Sutton, 'Let me lean back and survey the world, condemning it before it has the chance to condemn me.'[28] An earlier version of the same theme occurs when he says, 'By the way, don't mind my slandering friends behind their backs – I mean, you can't slander them to their faces, can you? That's how I look at it.'[29] Perhaps, too, he dislikes the figure of Art itself in some sense. Some of his earliest views of this figure, as they are expressed in the *apologia* poems in his 1944–50 working notebook, cast the figure of Literature as a hateful, pretentious patriarch who chides the poet but who does not understand him or his needs. In 'Reasons for Attendance' from *The Less Deceived*, art has become depersonalised into 'that lifted, rough-tongued bell' which is no longer directly menacing or uncomprehending (*CP*, 80). Here it is simply separate, and it primarily embodies the idea of individuality, and of individuating oneself not only from the ordinary people who mingle in a social throng (dancing 'Solemnly on the beat of happiness'), but even from other artists. 'It speaks; I hear; others may hear as well, / But not for me, nor I for them' (*CP*, 80). His anxieties and fears about not producing were enormous. One account, in a letter to Sutton, depicts the following imaginary scene: 'Every now and then a ghostly hand grabs the seat of my trousers and hauls me several feet off the ground, and I hear a ghostly voice say "Philip Larkin! You and your sharp sensitivity to words! What have you written since August 1945? Cock all!"' The end of the nightmare vision is also terrifying: 'The hand then releases me and I come a terrible bash on the cobbles.'[30]

In terms of culture, as in relation to other people, Larkin's poet figure remains separated between the poles of popular art and high art, or, in the case of jazz, between vernacular music and art music: he stands watching through the window with his nose pressed against the glass. He is not entirely at home in the world of high culture, but he is not simply a low-brow either, with unconsidered opinions. Larkin might well stress the ordinariness of his own poetry because this fulfils his ideal of art – that which captures an essential piece of life itself and conveys that experience or thought to others – and because it also constitutes his way of rebelling against previously existing forms. The fact that he is linked with The Movement poets of the 1950s reinforces the possibility that some general notion of the necessity for a backlash against modernism had emerged. This became a way of individuating himself as a poet and of finding a particular voice as an artist, even in separating himself from other contemporary poets. In his early writing, he tended not only to imitate other authors, but to identify strongly with them; at one point, he casts himself dramatically as Katherine Mansfield's 'illegitimate son'.[31] In the same way that jazz musicians took up music written by a specific composer and altered it, Larkin wrote variations on the work of other poets by directly imitating it.

At the same time, Larkin's rebellion against modernism as a whole may have been a necessary stage in his development; a means of clearing away an influence that had become too demanding or oppressive. This reaction seems to suit him temperamentally also. In writing defiantly against what he disliked and in favour of what he did like, he seemed to direct a great deal of energy towards an effort to individuate himself. Strong language thus became liberating as he asserted his own views. I suspect that the exercise of writing prose reviews both of books and of jazz records stimulated his poetry as well, since it provided another way to define his self-consciously philistine bent and to explore its implications. In addition, it was a means of asserting himself and of influencing the way in which we perceive genres – if only slightly. Writing a column of reviews of jazz records elevated the art to a higher importance; publishing the reviews as a book would tend to do so even further. By consulting and considering primarily his own feelings about other art works, Larkin could liberate himself indirectly from potentially oppressive critics who would accuse his own poetry of lacking seriousness. Much of his prose writing is spent in defending himself and his views, thus perhaps clearing space for his own creative writing. In addition, his continuing fascination throughout *Required Writing* with other writers' creative processes suggests that he might have been drawn toward seeing how other artists solved their problems. His own struggles with the 'ghostly hand' which throws him physically onto the cobblestones certainly made him sympathetic to other authors' plights. The philistine bent thus provides a way of addressing these problems. Great reserves of underlying emotion drive his work, and in the remainder of this chapter, I would like to consider Larkin's views of art as expressed forcefully in his jazz essays, his critical writings, his anthology for Oxford University Press, and finally his use of coarse language in his poetry. In most cases, the strong language he uses seems both to give direct expression to his emotions and to be liberating, even exhilarating. Perhaps, like Don Quixote, Larkin went so far as to create enemies where there were none, in order to argue vehemently with them; in any case, the exercise seems to have stimulated his thinking.

Larkin loved jazz for its rhythm (he had a passion for playing the drums when he was a boy) and above all for its instinctual, emotive qualities. He could *feel* things when he listened to it. He writes approvingly in 1965 of the jazz of twenty-five years earlier: 'All the emphasis was on feeling, emotional communication, sincerity' (*AWJ*, 137). Good music to Larkin is most often music which evokes a physical response, such as toe-tapping or whistling, or strong emotion, as in the following description of a particular piece: 'it is Armstrong's staggering and economical sincerity that makes this kind of number succeed. Indeed, it brought tears to my eyes' (*AWJ*, 119). A stunning example of this participation in the music – and sheer abandonment to it – occurs in a letter which Larkin wrote to Sutton while in his late teens. He describes playing a record of 'Dallas Blues', and adds:

> If you strayed into our hall, and stood outside the drawing room door, you might hear something like this . . .
> '(moan, moan) . . . yowse suh! . . . give, Louis, give! . . . (moan, groan) . . . man, jam dat ole horn like nobodies bizzness! . . . Yeah! . . . (moan, grunt) . . . slap dat bass, you niggah! . . . In the groove there! . . . (lament, shiek) . . . take it away, youleader-man![32]

His final exhortation consists of: 'Jive it up, boys! Get hot! Wow-oooo-owowow-ooooop!!!'[33] Jazz is, above all, great fun – even when experienced alone, by oneself, with the effects described later to a friend. Much of his satisfaction with it comes also from being able to judge and analyse it; the 'jiving' is followed by a long critique of the piece, and he declares at the end '(If I couldn't review as well as

Mike, I'd eat my hat!)'[34] Both of these strains – participating in and reviewing the music – continued in Larkin's later life, since he did eventually undertake to review jazz records in a column for the *Daily Telegraph* from 1961–1971; and the enthusiasm lasted until late in Larkin's life. In a BBC radio interview, Michael Bowen describes listening enthusiastically to jazz records with Larkin: 'He couldn't possibly sit still when the Count Basie Orchestra was in full flight, almost capering, outside himself, I mean a fat jitterbug, if you like'.[35]

Another high value in jazz for Larkin is the referentiality of words to emotions, a corollary to sincerity. He writes enthusiastically of this quality in Billie Holliday:

> To me she is best when singing a tune because she likes it and words because she believes them, while a few good sidemen take care of the improvising in the background. When in 'The Man I Love' on the first side she sings 'We'll build a little home', the shiver the listener feels is produced not by any significant-form attitude that regards the tune and lyrics as raw material to be improved but by an absolutely straight treatment that convinces him that Billie means simply that when she meets the man she loves they will be happy ever after. (*AWJ*, 148)

This performance seems to him to embody the directness of expression which Larkin so much valued in art, as Billie Holliday 'convinces' the listener that she means what she sings – an achievement all the more remarkable given the pain she experienced in her life.

In attempting to define the appeal of jazz, (a passion which he shared with Larkin), Kingsley Amis suggests the following perspectives: 'A form ideally suited to those with enough – but no more – music in them to respond intensely to a few strong, simple effects? A world of romance with no guide, no senior person to point the way?'[36] All of these thoughts are involved in understanding this connection – and the lack of a 'senior person to point the way' parallels Larkin's contempt for *Beowulf* and all the weight of traditional reading while up at Oxford – and his preference for D. H. Lawrence. Several elements in jazz suggest the sense of emotional abandon which Larkin was seeking early in his writing career. For one thing, it exemplified continual, fertile creativity; in vernacular music, the endless variations mean that the same melody would never be heard in the same way twice. Improvisation also meant sheer emotive expression on the part of the musician. In jazz, the work of art is virtually recreated with each performance. And jazz also stood for a whole complex of supportive camaraderie which would give substance to that work (musical background for the soloist, supporting 'sideman', a distinctly all-male group) and for a daring, adventurous life-style (a subculture of alcohol and drugs).

It is curious to find Larkin passionate about something as essentially foreign as jazz. This does not accord with his repeated insistence on the virtues of England and his abhorrence of 'abroad'. At the same time, it is possible that jazz appealed to him for exactly this reason: in its early context, at least, it represents 'Everyone making love and going shares – ' in his poem 'For Sidney Bechet'; namely, the giddiness of free sex, a free life and a breezy American disregard for convention (*CP*, 83). Initially he did not see it as distinctly American, as he explains in an interview: 'I listened to bands like that [Payne, Cotton, Roy] for an awfully long time without realising that there was such a thing as *American* jazz' (*RW*, 50). In several of his later reviews, however, Larkin constantly refers to this distinction in terms of the music's nationality and origin; jazz is proclaimed to be 'probably the most-loved thing ever to come out of America' (*AWJ*, 82). Yet at the same time it symbolises something larger, in his view: 'From being American folk music it has become world folk music' (*AWJ*, 82). This is not, of course, an accurate distinction on Larkin's part, since jazz music has an identifiable composer, which folk music does not; but designating jazz as folk music makes it represent for him a kind of grass-roots immediacy and popular appeal. His praise for musicians he admires is enthusiastic, though he is markedly sceptical of any possible excess in emotion on the part of a performer. He is quite caustic in his remarks about the jacket copy of 'A Love Supreme', which includes 'a signed statement by Coltrane that this album is "an attempt to say 'THANK YOU, GOD' through our work." Let us hope this is the whim of the A & R man, for otherwise it would point to a degree of self-seriousness most inimical to an artist' (*AWJ*, 142). This is an ironic kind of complaint, in that Larkin only allows the jazz musician to emote musically but not verbally, a distinction which suggests in part why the genre of music appealed to him so strongly. Jazz seems to provide an outlet for the expression of strong, even violent emotion, without the embarrassment of personal meaning being attached to it.

Although Larkin generally discounts the academic world in which he moves (All Souls is referred to slyly in a jazz review as 'an institution' with a 'somewhat intimidating address'), he enjoys making covert and mocking reference to its terminology (*AWJ*, 265). In a review entitled 'The Parker legend', Larkin observes that 'The tenth anniversary of the death of Charlie Parker cannot but provoke a look, however brief, at what in another context would be called the state of Parker studies' (*AWJ*, 135). Yet despite this ironic tone, he remained fascinated with these musicians' private lives and public reputations. Larkin approved of giving praise when praise was due. Tributes to Ellington and Armstrong seem to him entirely appropriate, and are written with a sense of near reverence:

> it is always a matter for rejoicing when an artist reaches three-score years and ten without having given up and with his international reputation still undiminished, and in a world where fashion and money and temperament take a ruthless toll of its servants it is appropriate to salute these two great Americans and the tenacity which enabled them to fulfil their destinies. (*AWJ*, 267)

Again, much of the huge significance of jazz for Larkin lay in his admiration for the expressiveness of the artists who performed and continually recreated it. Throughout these reviews, Larkin is often keenly interested in individual artists and in their reputations. He shows a great breadth of knowledge of 'who's who' in jazz, both earlier players and contemporary ones, and highly recommends John Chilton's *Who's Who in Jazz* for its inclusiveness and methodical completeness (*AWJ*, 263). He clearly expects the fellow jazz aficionado to be both serious and well-informed. And this stresses the personal, intimate aspect of jazz which at times amounts almost to hero worship.

Perhaps most important of all, jazz represents for Larkin that means of access to the unconscious for which he so yearned. In a letter to Sutton, he defines feeling as a 'rational function' and sensation as 'irrational: the mere receiving of an impression'. Ordinary sensation is 'recognisable – only in cases where it is suppressed and disregarded does it assume a violent form – such as jazz. I don't know how an ordinary person hears jazz.'[37] This formulation suggests that jazz takes a 'violent form' because it is repressed psychic energy, and therefore expressive of raw emotion. One of Larkin's main desires at this point in his life was to tap his emotions for creative purposes – he writes also to Sutton that D. H. Lawrence was admirable because 'no good writer (i.e. DHL [sic] is afraid of his emotion.'[38] What is curious about this endeavour is that

Larkin had ambivalent feelings about the value of the unconscious mind. When he started to read Jung, after Freud, he wrote to Sutton: 'The unconscious, instead of being a garbage-heap of shame and guilt, is the fountain of life, and contains the healing powers of everyone. How to get at them I still am not sure. But I live in hopes.'[39] Still, regardless of what it contains, the unconscious seems to him essential for creativity.

The helpful effect of jazz on Larkin was that it enabled him to get in touch with his emotions – and to participate in the excitement of the music through toe-tapping and capering about the room. The other side of this situation is that this particular kind of expression means getting in touch with raw emotion rather than processing his feelings and gaining insight into them. He can feel through jazz, but not in a way that changes him. Jazz represents a lack of control; but, significantly, when jazz itself seemed to go out of his control he was furious. His gallant battle against modernism as he perceived it in jazz (the post-Parker era) seems a *cri de coeur* reflecting a genuinely personal loss of some sort of essential life-line.

A constant theme in his reviews is his denunciation of modernism – and this stems from his heart as much as from his head. The introduction to *All What Jazz* is his primary manifesto, and seems almost frantic in its sense of loss: 'After Pound! After Picasso! There could hardly have been a conciser summary of what I don't believe about art' (*AWJ*, 23). As Larkin himself is shrewdly aware, his personal commitment to an ideal often impinges upon what he feels ought to be his proper public demeanour; the lines which follow the 'conciser summary' caution with half apology (which is *not* an apology) that 'The reader may here have the sense of having strayed into a private argument' (*AWJ*, 23). Yet many of his views on art stem from exactly this principle: one's own opinions should be brought into play when one is trying to discern the value of art – because, paradoxically, art matters so much. Thus in addition to larger cultural issues, there is a certain streak of nostalgia in all of this. Larkin at times conveys the impression of a sensible, rational, nineteenth-century man living on alone into the twentieth century, taking a lonely stand against freakish innovation and increasing cultural and moral darkness. He continually evokes a vanished past which lies just out of reach. The vintage jazz records to which he has recourse are a reminder of past glories, which can never come again. And it worries him so much that he now, conversely, must protest that he does still maintain a personal commitment to the music. In the 1984 'Footnote to the Second Edition' of *All What Jazz*, he rejects the notion that the book casts him as 'a disliker rather than a liker'.

> I still insist I love jazz: the great coloured pioneers and their eager white disciples, and the increasingly remote world that surrounded their music, dance halls, derby hats, band buses, tuxedos, monogrammed music-stands, the shabby recording studios where they assembled, and the hanging honeycomb microphones that saved it all for us. (*AWJ*, 31)

His rhetorical strategy here blends detachment and sorrow. Larkin gives this such an ironic and belligerent tone that one would hesitate to see nostalgia in his view; and these qualities in his writing tend to cover this sentimental streak effectively. At the same time, it is slightly odd that he should seem to love the culture of jazz musicians almost more than its musical sounds; and it suggests again that the relative freedom which he observes them living out appeals to him strongly.

Significantly, jazz is connected not only with another place but with another time – and that a personal one, as it symbolises Larkin's youth; the review entitled 'All what jazz?' begins with the wry comment: 'Comes inevitably the month when the new records seemingly offer nothing but platitude, prolixity, pretension. Jazz, the reviewer thinks, is dying – or is it himself?' (*AWJ*, 115).

But most curious of all is the tremendous sense of constraint which Larkin felt while composing these reviews; he strove for politeness when writing about a subject (jazz) which he loved in a manifestation (modern jazz) which he hated. In his Introduction he describes his initial plan, which was to praise everything which was presented to him for review, but this was soon dropped because of his growing conviction that jazz as he knew it was dead. Echoing those 'two principal themes of modernism', as he defines them, Larkin himself moved from 'mystification' to 'outrage' (*AWJ*, 23–24). His final appraisal of the reviews as a group included 'the amusement – at least, for me – [of] watching truthfulness break in, despite my initial resolve' (*AWJ*, 25). This tension between saying what he thought he was expected to say and saying what he felt ('using [one's] eyes and ears and [understanding] to report pleasure and discomfort' (*AWJ*, 24)) seems to underlie many of the reviews reprinted in the book. In a fundamental sense, writing *All What Jazz* seems to have been the reverse of the liberating experience of freely offering his own opinions. Yet at the same time, 'truthfulness' does break in fairly often; at the least, Larkin's tone always carries great conviction.

His analysis of the regression – finally the 'death' – of jazz is particularly significant in that it bears out in another context besides the poetry Larkin's insistence on the importance of the audience in relation to art and the artist. In his view, when this connection became severed, jazz began to decline: 'The tension between artist and audience in jazz slackened when the Negro stopped wanting to entertain the white man, and then the audience as a whole, with the end of the Japanese war and the beginning of television, didn't in any case particularly want to be entertained in that way any longer' (*AWJ*, 24). Almost as if in search of others to share his opinions, Larkin seems to feel the need to define his own audience, the readers of these reviews; he pictures them in poignantly romantic terms:

> Sometimes I imagine them, sullen fleshy inarticulate men, stockbrokers, sellers of goods, living in 30-year-old detached houses among the golf courses of Outer London, husbands of ageing and bitter wives ... men whose first coronary is coming like Christmas; who drift, loaded helplessly with commitments and obligations and necessary observances, into the darkening avenues of age and incapacity, deserted by everything that once made life sweet. (*AWJ*, 28–9)

His final comment sums up all that art – and an art critic/jazz reviewer – should do for the audience in this scheme: 'These [readers] I have tried to remind of the excitement of jazz, and tell where it may still be found' (*AWJ*, 29).[40]

Thus in *All What Jazz* the sense of a like-minded audience and of *shared* appreciation is crucial, just as at Oxford, jazz became for Larkin and many of his friends 'part of the private joke of existence' (*AWJ*, 17). A whistled tune overheard in a college bath cubicle became shorthand for camaraderie, for a shared outlook, possibly even a subversiveness or irreverence held in common. But it is also very strange that he should seem to feel so defensive about this audience of middle-aged men; his lyrical description almost betrays insecurity. If he really felt kinship with them, he would not have to create them so vividly. As in much of his writing, the world outside seems faintly hostile – even in what is on the surface a warm, emotional appeal.

Throughout these reviews, Larkin seems to write for two different and opposing kinds of audience. First, he writes for those readers who are open-minded towards or receptive to contemporary jazz; those whom he strove not to offend by substituting '"adventurous" for "excruciating"', and "colourful" for "viciously absurd" in a thoroughly professional manner' (*AWJ*, 28). Second, he writes for those old Oxford cronies whom he feels certain will agree with him about the 'nightmare' of the contemporary scene and the horror of the new generation of impudent youth ('We're gonna do you, Dad'). These men ('inarticulate' on their own) are the readers to whom Larkin appeals and for whom he speaks – and with whom he symbolically shares a remote past. His frustration with the current state of the art is evident, as he observes a fundamental shift: 'the sort of emotion the music was trying to evoke seemed to have changed' (*AWJ*, 19). Yet what gives the reviews an added tension is the uncertainty about whether the readers will agree with him or not. Perhaps his final envisioning of them en masse is a kind of creative wishful thinking; surely someone out there will be moved by the sweetness of remembered youth, which is recalled by the jazz of earlier and better times.

Jazz is in many ways a sophisticated taste rather than a philistine one – though the two forms are not mutually exclusive. In a *New York Review of Books* essay, E. J. Hobsbawm points out that 'the public for it has been tiny: far smaller than the public for classical music', although historical jazz is becoming increasingly more accessible and popular.[41] Yet there remains this problem of radical change in the art form itself; Larkin documents a cut-off point in his own musical tastes (something he certainly shares with a number of jazz enthusiasts); he embraces early jazz and reviles its post-Parker manifestation. His relationship with the art form is a complex one, changing from the joy he derived from it in his Oxford years through the frustration yet nostalgic comfort he expressed in the collection of essays which he wrote in the 1960s. Characteristically extreme in his reactions, he veers between admiration and hatred, transport and regret. Always, his is a deeply felt personal response; 'Jazz, the reviewer thinks, is dying – or is it himself?' (*AWJ*, 115).

As in *All What Jazz*, where Larkin divides jazz into early and late, alive and dying, in many of the book reviews collected in *Required Writing* he also tends to seize on extremes and to use all his ingenuity to exploit them. This led one irritated book critic to confer upon him the title of 'The opinionated poet'.[42] Yet on the whole, this seems an unwarranted complaint, setting aside the initial objection, that a poet might well have opinions; Larkin's essays may tend to be impressionistic, but on the other hand, he is primarily writing as a fellow artist who alternately admires and criticises other artists' works and who above all sympathises with their problems in writing. In *Required Writing*, then, Larkin writes about literature as a fellow writer of literature as well as a reader, though primarily as the latter. As in his jazz reviews, his impressionistic style of criticism stems from an impulse to *define* what he himself intuitively likes. Many of the pieces insist on a personal affinity with a given work as a starting point for evaluation of it. The essay on Stevie Smith's poetry, for example, begins with the announcement that Larkin fortuitously discovered a copy of her volume *Not Waving but Drowning*, and consequently bought several volumes as Christmas gifts for friends. This way of introducing the subject of the review suggests that he feels he is going out on a limb in championing such a book – and that he willing to do so, both in the domain of private relationships and of public essay form. He wants to define and explain his admiration, although in the end this particular experiment went wrong; the friends were 'bothered to know whether I seriously expected them to admire it. The more I insisted that I did, the more suspicious they became. An unfortunate episode' (*RW*, 153).

What many of these essays suggest is Larkin's readiness, even eagerness, to rely on his own discernment in matters of literary taste. Moreover, the Stevie Smith episode proves that he is right to insist on his own views, since *no one's* mind can potentially be changed. His own enthusiasm may well not be reciprocated, and perhaps it is best not even to share it with friends in the first place. Such mutual misunderstanding comprises an 'unfortunate episode'. Nonetheless, he did persist in following this course of reliance on his own literary intuition. He chose his subjects carefully; each of Larkin's essays has a peculiar ring to it because it seems to be a firm private conviction at last made public. His tendency to champion writers whom he liked stems in part from his delight in taking a firm (preferably unorthodox) line. The contemporary literary community, with its growing formal organisation and inherent power of critical judgement may well have intimidated him in a way he did not like. His markedly conservative literary views may also stem from his genuine kindliness and his distress at seeing anyone whose work he liked bullied.

In his essays on figures such as Betjeman, Hardy and Housman, Larkin seems to sense a hostile and unreceptive audience and to declare a sort of cold war against them which precludes mutual dialogue. He tends to defend his own view-points rather than seek to persuade his readers to share them. In addition, (and much like a typical academic) he seems to want most of all to clear a space for his own work by subtly suggesting that no one else has really done it properly. In a piece on Thomas Hardy's novels, he even goes so far as to advertise a vacancy in the title: 'Wanted: good Hardy critic'. Though he often despises academic writing, Larkin has clearly come to grips with it and has read at least some important critical books. But his starting point always remains the same, the work of art itself. When writing a review of an academic book on *Tess of the D'Urbervilles*, for instance, he makes a point of reading the novel again himself. The scholarly book on Hardy which he is reviewing seems so notably muddle-headed that Larkin can easily be accused of setting up a straw man – and indeed, much of his critical writing seems to do just this.

Still, in addition to pungent phrasing and occasionally brash declarations, his reviews often display great subtlety and finesse. When discussing Tennyson's poetry, for instance, he makes fun of it indirectly by citing an example of someone else's irreverence, and then placing himself in the position of reluctantly yet gleefully agreeing with this judgement. In connection with 'the repeated eponym in "The Ballad of Oriana"', the first lines of which are 'They should have stabb'd me where I lay, / Oriana!', Larkin says the following: 'It was Mr Robert Graves, I think, who suggested the substitution of the words "bottom upwards" for the refrain. This is disgraceful, but it is the kind of mockery Tennyson invited' (*RW*, 185). Similarly, at times Larkin insists on plain speech in an exaggeratedly philistine sort of way. His discussion of Marvell's poetry casts involved academic readings in an ironically simplifying light; a lengthy explication of the 'vegetable love' in Marvell's 'To His Coy Mistress' elicits the plain-speaking man's response: 'Another reader might simply think that "vegetable" was a good adjective for something that grows slowly' (*RW*, 247). In describing what he perceives to be a fruitless dialectical argument about the poem, Larkin pits critics against each other as though they were rugby teams: 'Certainly critic quarrelled with critic on what could or should be read into Marvell's lines: Leavis with Bateson, Douglas Bush with Cleanth Brooks, [*et al.*] (*RW*, 248). This is, a critic might feel, rather a slanted characterisation of the workings of scholarship; yet at the same time, it seems possible that Larkin is writing less on Marvell's behalf than on his own, as a contemporary poet, whose work will potentially be subjected to the same sort of tedious analysis. His reviews are nothing if not personal, both as they express his own opinions and as they obscurely defend his own work, which is firmly based on these opinions.

In part, these essays are interesting just because they show what (and to some extent how) Larkin thinks. If they succeed for his readers, it is because they express the projection of a ludicrous super-ego onto the world. At times, one would like to simply denounce the opposition. But these pieces are also interesting because of the peculiar insight which he brings to bear on the works of other writers. Larkin has an uncanny knack of pinpointing the significant event which triggered another artist's creativity, and he often seems fascinated by the question of what motivates someone to write. A stanza of Francis Thompson's, for instance, is cast as a metaphor for Thompson's entire life, which is characterised as being an unsuccessful 'attempt to get himself out of bed' (RW, 122). In another such description, Edward Thomas is seen as having been liberated to write when an unexpected means of release from domestic cares occurred; this calls forth from Larkin the comment: 'How this stalemate of temperament and circumstance suddenly produced a unique body of poems is a matter for marvelling' (RW, 189). On occasion, Larkin's judgements are unreasonably harsh; Rupert Brooke seems most unfairly judged as an opportunistic businessman, when he in fact wrote fluently and well. (One hesitates to ascribe part of this reaction to professional jealousy, but Brooke seems to have possessed exactly the sort of dazzling young talent calculated to enrage a fellow craftsman.) At times Larkin polarises varying ideas excessively, as in his dialectical, opposing views of W. H. Auden, whose work he splits into two entirely different and conflicting periods, the latter of which occasions 'a sharp division of opinion about his poetic stature' (RW, 123). The title of the review, 'What's become of Wystan?', clearly suggests Larkin's own opinion on the matter. This dichotomy reflects the main weakness in Larkin's critical essays, namely, their insistence on simple views which can cancel each other out rather than allowing a multiplicity of view-points.

At the same time, though, Larkin seems acutely conscious of the continual reshaping of an artist's reputation in light of subsequent knowledge, and of the value of thinking about that reputation over a longer period. Here he allows for a process of change and for discussion by many people. In his discussion of Wilfred Owen, Larkin thinks that a fifty-year period of assessment is needed to allow views about the artist, if not about his work, to evolve. This seems to him to be true especially in the case of an author who dies young: 'The work is published, and will not be added to, and we start making up our minds about it: the life, on the other hand, is guarded by widow, family, friends, trustees, and fifty years may go by before a total picture is presented' (*RW*, 228). While the work stands as something which we make up our minds about, the life of the poet is seen as existing in a flux. In this essay, he goes on to suggest several compelling perspectives on Owen's life and poetry; and far from being excessively opinionated, he stresses the mystery that remains: 'Somewhere behind [the poetry] was a human problem that even after fifty years we are a long way from understanding' (*RW*, 239). In many ways it is the deliberately divided scheme which appeals to Larkin, as in his appreciation of Montherlant's depiction of a male character in a novel, a review which reveals genuine admiration for clear distinctions: 'Montherlant's principal dichotomy – men this, women that – has virtually disappeared from our unisex world' (*RW*, 261). Yet at the same time, Larkin often allows for the unaccountability of certain feelings or the difficulty of interpreting certain poems or ideas. He never insists on his own views as the only possible right ones – or that anyone else should adopt them if still unpersuaded. His pervadingly impressionistic criticism – or the emphasis on what he feels as a reader – is often a private argument made public, though never an insistent one.

For the most part, *Required Writing* bears out Larkin's stated views on what art and criticism of it should be. He primarily consults his own opinions; as he formulates this process in the introduction to *All What Jazz*, the operating criteria is simply: 'As it enters the ear, does it come in like broken glass or does it come in like honey?' (*AWJ*, 28). His emphasis is on that which is of value, and of value to him.

Part of his agenda seems to be to reshape the literary canon in terms of his intuitive response to it. The fact that much of his energy was directed towards championing conservative literary taste is both ironic and subversive. Again, in this kind of situation, Larkin can go outside the accepted body of knowledge to that which is fundamentally more interesting or desirable. He seems to have enjoyed playing the role of a radical, outspoken voice for conservative, even reactionary, taste. In line with his intensely personal response to literature, much of his overstatement at times stems from his kindness to friends who were writers. When he received copies of three of Pym's novels after a long period during which her work remained unpublished he wrote: 'It really is a deep joy to me to contemplate them – not *unmixed* joy, because I want to set my teeth in the necks of various publishers and shake them like rats – but a great pleasure, nonetheless.'[43] In matters of taste he might well be considered unorthodox, but when he wrote to Barbara Pym that he would 'sooner read a new BP than a new JA [Jane Austen]!' he was probably being serious.[44] He vigorously proclaims in letters to Pym that she ought indeed to have an audience for her novels: 'not everyone yearns to read of S. Africa or Negro homosexuals or the woes of Professional Rugby League Players. Or not exclusively.'[45]

Larkin's accompanying perfectionism also affects these essays on various topics. He is never slow to point out other artists' limitations – to challenge, and even to argue about, various weak points. His admiration for any given writer is usually somewhat qualified, lest he give the impression of being too gullible. Also, if he professes a grudging admiration or respect for someone, his views then seem not to be facile. Larkin gives reasons for his critical judgements; but at the same time, the emotional power which drives them should not be discounted. It is, moreover, part of his strategy; he seems to proceed as though confident that if he bares his soul and shares his private reactions, the reader cannot help but be swayed by his certain convictions – and if not share them, at least tolerate them. Larkin, then, wants to persuade his readers of some particular point of view – that Hardy is generally misunderstood and undervalued, that the poetry of Ogden Nash (though popular) has several unappreciated virtues.

If 'MIDDLEBROW LITERARY CHAT RULES OK' in these essays, it is because Larkin conceived of himself as telling the truth about what he felt. And this remark plus his introduction to *Required Writing* suggest that he thought of himself as a 'common man' sort of reader – yet this is not strictly true, of course. If he was busy denouncing *Beowulf* and *The Faerie Queene* while up at Oxford, he was also in the process of getting a first there as well. Robert Crawford reminds us that 'Larkin's statements are not to be taken at face value.'[46] The 'middle-brow' line is a pose of sorts. It seems possible that Larkin took it in order to forestall criticism of his views, and also in order to feel ironically superior to those who would challenge them. Heavy academic dudes won't bother to mess with him if he protests that he is just a regular guy. At the same time, he can quarrel with their work, all the while insisting that he has no official platform from which to address them. Perhaps Amis captures this aspect of Larkin best in this description of his energy and verve: 'his company brought a jovial reassurance, a sense that the fools and charlatans, the Pounds and Picassos and many of their living heirs were doomed by their own absurdity.'[47]

An example of the results of Larkin's reliance on his own literary instincts is the anthology of twentieth-century poetry which he compiled for Oxford University Press, and which was published in 1973. The invitation to edit such a volume was considered an honour, and must have been gratifying; as Grevel Lindop observes: 'Oxford Books of this and that are felt to have a kind of canonical status, embodying the doctrine of their generation on whatever genre they represent.'[48] In effect, the editing of the anthology provided an official platform from which to reshape the literary canon. Larkin accordingly joked about the book while work on it was in progress, stressing its difficulty and importance. As he wrote to Barbara Pym when contemplating the task: 'Behind that [other work] stands an anthology for OUP, menacing, profound.'[49] Once the book was published he absolutely did not apologise for any aspect of it and many of his comments reveal that he was proud of the end result. The way in which he compiled it bears out his earlier ideal of thinking for oneself: in response to an interview question from Anthony Thwaite about how he worked on the volume, Larkin replied, 'Well, in simplistic terms, I read all the poetry produced in this century, which took about four and a half years, and then picked out the bits I liked the best.'[50] Ironically, he tends to make this endeavour sound deliberately prosaic and ordinary. However, he emphasises in another interview that he feels his approach to be unique: 'Most people make anthologies out of other anthologies' (RW, 73). He also stresses that he tried to represent common consensus as well, as he tells Thwaite: 'I tried throughout my selection to put my own taste reasonably in the background.'[51]

These two descriptions of his editorial methods are, in fact, contradictory, since he claims in one context to have chosen what he liked best and in the other to have put his own tastes aside. Yet taken together, these statements suggest that Larkin worked in a middle ground between these views; he seems to believe that he can compile a representative collection by trusting primarily in his own judgement. He also comments on the difficulty of choosing that poetry which seems most worthy of inclusion in the book without a general concensus of literary opinion: 'The difficulty with doing an anthology of poems of your own time . . . is that you haven't got the help of that greatest anthologist, time. You're really just bashing away by instinct.'[52] It is true that the idea of compiling the anthology irritated him because of the necessary constraints of politeness which it imposed. He describes his anticipation of the project to Pym with some distaste: 'The Ox. Bk. is starting to worry me, (yes, I start from scratch), partly owing to my strong dislike of a great many poets of the century who are reckoned to be good, and not really knowing what I am supposed to be doing.'[53]

In due course, his choice irritated several other people. A letter to Pym on publication of the book shows Larkin's fatalistic dread of reviews, which were in fact mixed: 'From Thursday to Sunday inclusive you won't be able to avoid long paragraphs of abuse of me, in everything you pick up.'[54] What the anthology achieves, though, is to provide yet another manifestation of Larkin's basic views about art: the book in question should please its readers (here largely composed of Larkin himself as a representative reader, and suggesting a confidence in assuming that role); and its choice of poems should not rely on the reputation of a given poet, but on intrinsic merit. The kind of bullying which exalts 'major' authors in favour of (or to the exclusion of) 'minor' ones is set aside here in Larkin's direct appeal to the individual poem itself.

In response to Thwaite's query about his preface to the Oxford anthology, Larkin firmly disclaimed any special abilities or any desire to use his position as editor in order to make a statement about poetry in the abstract: 'I'm not a theorist, I'm not a critic, I'm not an academic. In a sense, the selection itself is my preface, if that's not too metaphysical. I have no real desire to lay down the law about anything.'[55]

It is tempting to take this judgement as final, and to discount Larkin's numerous, very firm remarks as a critic and reviewer. In some sense, many of the judgements in *Required Writing* seem sufficiently direct and powerful to make one conclude that Larkin is simply an opinionated bully himself, perhaps eager to engage in fisticuffs with other bullies who lay down the law. But what remain intriguing are the possible reasons behind this habitual aggressiveness. From one point of view, the essays' apparent finality and unanswerableness tend to repel criticism; it seems pointless to challenge Larkin's views because it is clear that he refuses to be convinced otherwise. Further, his forthright style is often calculated to provoke a definite response from his readers. He delights in an intellectual 'punch-up.' Yet at the same time, Larkin's certainty, his belligerence even, is in part a pose which he adopts in order to compensate for some measure of private self-doubt and anxiety. It is undercut by consistent self-mockery, often carrying out a deliberate strategy to get his own licks in before you can get at him. This constant sending up of himself gives a subversive element to his work, contrasting with his grand pronouncements. The tone of aggrieved personal resentment in which he pronounces many of his strongest judgements has led some people to dismiss him as a silly old buffer. However, it could be argued that Larkin is taking a calculated risk; in adopting this 'opinionated' stance he is trying to allow the non-expert, non-academic, thoughtful reader, artist and common man in him to voice their views. This is a continuation of the strategy which he first outlined while still at Oxford in a letter to Sutton: 'Let me lean back and survey the world, condemning it before it has the chance to condemn me.'[56]

Although Larkin will often mock himself, he reacts violently if anyone else seems to be laughing at him. When nettled in the course of an interview, he can bark out a formidable response. 'I begin to wonder how old you are, Anthony, because during the war Pudney's poems were very, very popular', begins one answer to Anthony Thwaite.[57] A question about reading poetry in a foreign language evokes an explosion of impatience: 'If that glass thing over there is a window, then it isn't a *Fenster* or a *fenêtre* or whatever. *Hautes fenêtres*, my God!' (*RW*, 69). And displeasure with an interviewer occasionally surfaces as well: 'What questions you ask', he wrote to the *Paris Review* interviewer, who was questioning him through the post – the two men never actually met (*RW*, 62). In fact, interviews were indeed very strenuous for him, as he wrote to Pym; 'they take up the hell of a time and are gruelling experiences.'[58] The *Observer* interview he described as 'very trying – questions about why hadn't I got married, what were my politics, did I think love caused unhappiness, etc. I writhed like a worm on a hook ... Oh dear.'[59] Oakes observes astutely in his interview with Larkin that he is 'personally modest, but he is blazingly proud of his craft.'[60] And this is of a piece with his determination to deprecate himself before anyone else can do so.

A characteristic instance of inventive self-mockery appears in a letter to Barbara Pym, in which Larkin arranges their meeting for the first time at the Randolph Hotel in Oxford. Larkin described his appearance as follows: 'I'm sure we shall recognise each other by progressive elimination, i.e., eliminating all the progressives. I am tall and bald and heavily spectacled and deaf, but I can't predict what I shall have on.'[61] The first part is so assured that his lack of ability to predict his clothing is comic. Similarly, his reported description of himself as looking 'like a bald salmon' is engagingly shrewd and naive – a pre-emptive strike at his opponents.[62]

What this pose reflects, then, is Larkin's immense sense of irony. It imparts security to adopt an unvarying stance, to proclaim a firm view-point and then to stick to it. A sweeping statement, such as 'Down with modernism', thus becomes both true for Larkin – he believes it in some sense, to be sure – and yet it is also a way of satisfying some need to express outrage and a firmly held belief. Continually creating dialectical arguments is an exhilarating rhetorical strategy; such extreme statements also parody Larkin's views and those held by his antagonists. Thus the limiting, narrow impulse that sometimes characterises Larkin's poetry actually stems from an immense, raging energy. It is his superhuman effort to keep life in order that makes his prose so firmly opinionated and his poetry so clear and forceful and precise. It is a radical effort of will, made against the overwhelming temptation to submit to melancholy and apathy.

The juxtaposition of clearly stated opinions and seething emotion underneath suggests a kind of complex double life, or, to return to a point made earlier, huge pressure like that experienced by Dixon in Amis' *Lucky Jim*. In the novel, the character gets rid of as much tension as he can through making faces or other inarticulate gestures, and these faces are an intensification and an expression of his feelings about others or about his situation. Larkin in his poetry also adopts something of this same approach by covertly creating an explosive atmosphere with a wealth of expletives. When Prof. Garnet Rees wrote to suggest an alternate ending to Larkin's commemorative poem for the fiftieth anniversary of the Brynmor Jones Library, Larkin replied by commending Prof. Rees's suggestion and confessing that he also had thought of other possible variations on the poem's closing lines – adducing one and confessing to 'others less printable'.[63] This reservoir of 'unprintable' material lurking just below the surface is a hidden source of energy; it occasionally breaks through in Larkin's poems, and when it does, it always produces some particular wrenching, dramatic effect.

On occasion, as in the poem entitled 'Love', it furthers the general impression of sparkling light verse written in a breathless Ogden Nash or Stevie Smith style. Very much like 'Self's the Man' in tone, 'Love' also expresses many of the same sentiments; in the first two stanzas, love is alternatively viewed as selfish and then unselfish, and as such it reflects one's value as a person:

> The difficult part of love
> Is being selfish enough,

Is having the blind persistence
To upset an existence
Just for your own sake.
What cheek it must take.

And then the unselfish side –
How can you be satisfied
Putting someone else first
So that you come off worst?
My life is for me.
As well ignore gravity.

(*CP*, 150)

The rhymes, as they occur close together in couplets, seem almost as though they forced the poet to make extreme statements. This is especially true with the feminine rhymes, such as 'persistence/existence', 'for me/gravity', and 'virtuous/most of us'. There is sheer playfulness in this arrangement of words which takes a serious subject – love and morality, vice and virtue – and pits various views against each other in a protest:

Still, vicious or virtuous,
Love suits most of us.
Only the bleeder found
Selfish this wrong way round
Is ever wholly rebuffed,
And he can get stuffed.

(*CP*, 150)

As in many of Larkin's firm statements, these two views cancel each other out. His facility with words seems matched by his dazzling ability to manipulate logic: in the first stanza, love is defined as selfish, while in the second stanza it is defined as unselfish and negated on exactly these grounds. After arguing the position out in the final stanza, the poem undercuts the whole problem, asserting that it does not matter anyway; 'Love suits most of us', and so there is no real point in the protest at all (*CP*, 150).

Yet there remains the 'bleeder' who is caught between. The poet's denunciation of him turns his rage in a particular direction, towards a particular figure. If someone still remains unconvinced that love is suitable despite its complex relationship with selfishness, he should be summarily dismissed: 'he can get stuffed' (*CP*, 150). In some terrifying sense, the poet is or could be that 'bleeder', as he himself is arguing about love's merits. And Larkin is often most inclined to villify those men who are possible variations of himself. Hence the same tactic occurs in the denunciation of the 'spectacled schoolteaching sod' and the 'shit in the shuttered château' who appear in 'Life with a Hole in It' (CP, 202). This bashing tends to be most severe in relation to figures who are alternatives to the speaker in the poem. Here neither alternative is good, though at least the poet himself rejoices in the fact that he has managed not to be the 'sod', if he can't be the 'shit' with the easy life. In a neurotic view of the world, no pleasure is conceivable or admissible without either pain or guilt – the 'sod' is saddled with pregnant wife and children, the irresponsible, alcoholic 'shit' *ought* to feel guilty if he does not actually do so. Coarse language can be directed against anyone whom the poet senses as an antagonist, like the 'old ratbags' who insist that he complains too much, or the philistine readers whom he attacks in 'Fiction and the Reading Public' (CP, 202). In fact, the fury expressed at the women in 'Life with a Hole in It' stems from the fact that they militate against and disapprove of strong language, which gives all the more reason to use it as a means of rebellion. Where the women would try to persuade him to retract his harsh, uncompromising stance, he regards silence on this point as an immoral altering of the truth:

> When I throw back my head and howl
> People (women mostly) say
> *But you've always done what you want,*
> *You always get your own way*
> – A perfectly vile and foul
> Inversion of all that's been.
>
> (CP, 202)

It is the 'old ratbags' who insist on polite, agreeable expression, and who, by doing this, want him not to tell the truth about his experience. The 'inversion' which they advocate as a suitable description means nothing less than a lie about reality. Still more compelling, the poet's expression of feeling and pain here is entirely raw and inarticulate; its purest expression is a 'howl'.

Larkin often writes about the predicament of the man who cannot express himself (either because he is inarticulate or because of the taboos of polite society) and uses it not only as a metaphor for pent-up rage but as a safety valve to relieve some of the pressure he feels.

Much of the bawdy language which actually appears in the poetry occurs solely within the realm of private thought. Thus these words suggest a seething inner turmoil, and they are meant to contrast sharply with the polite façade which the poet projects. The poet's response to the invitation of Warlock-Williams in *'Vers de Société'*, for instance, is an example of polite forbearance:

> *My wife and I have asked a crowd of craps*
> *To come and waste their time and ours: perhaps*
> *You'd care to join us? In a pig's arse, friend.*
>   (CP, 181)

The poet – too constrained by politeness to tell Warlock-Williams his instinctive response – keeps his reply to himself. And he does so because he is primarily motivated by fear of retaliation; he is ultimately too cautious to cut off his escape from solitude, (the evening spent alone) even when the alternative is the false camaraderie of *'société'* (a distasteful party at the Warlock-Williams'). Like Jim Dixon in Amis' *Lucky Jim*, Larkin's protagonist in the poem does not say directly what he means because he does not want to ruin the chance which he still has of remaining on equable terms with the outside world. Both figures are surprisingly cautious in this regard. Dixon actually writes down 'Ned Welch is a Soppy Fool with a Fase like A Pigs Ɓum', but he's careful only to do so on the steam-covered mirror in the Welches' bathroom.[64] He must remain on outwardly cordial terms with Professor Welch in order to keep his job, and only when this necessity disappears is he able to express his view of Welch and his family. When this chance finally appears, Dixon is suitably inarticulate: the end of the novel finds him doubled up 'in a howl of laughter' at the four of them.[65]

The Welches' 'Arty Weekend' at the beginning of the novel crystallises Dixon's horror of social gatherings and their attendant ennui. Significantly, Dixon's preference for solo drinking in a pub seems odd to people like Johns or Mrs Welch. Larkin's protagonists, however, could and do explain very well this yearning for solitude rather than the inevitable tension and non-conversation engendered by a social gathering. *'Vers de Société'* speaks feelingly about time flying 'Straight into nothingness by being filled / With forks and faces', and the penance and sheer boredom of '[catching] the drivel of some bitch / Who's read nothing but *Which*' (CP, 181).

Thus the speaker in *'Vers de Société'* finds himself in a similar position to that of Amis' Jim Dixon, who is constantly accepting invitations from Welch which by no means delight him. The speaker in Larkin's poem outwardly abases himself to Warlock-Williams in two polite responses: '*Dear Warlock-Williams: I'm afraid –* or '*Why, of course –*' both of which are gracious (*CP*, 181, 182). Part of the irony in the invitation is that Warlock-Williams (with a sinister parody of an upper-class name and clearly a blood-sucker too) starts out the exchange with vulgar language. In an attempt to appear sophisticated by being off-hand and at ease, he proposes an evening with a 'crowd of craps', certainly a rather debasing company, and deliberately devalued in a kind of inverted snobbism. These 'craps' no doubt appropriately put the poet in mind of a 'pig's arse', where one might expect to find them (*CP*, 181). Still, the poet only responds in kind to himself, and not out loud.

The rest of the poet's musings which follow are marked by a similar bluntness: he posits the inevitable existence at any given gathering of the 'bitch / Who's read nothing but *Which*'; and the ass with his 'fool research' (*CP*, 181). It is not even so much their presence at the party which enrages him, but the necessary effort of having to seem interested in their conversation. The system itself makes sincerity (i.e., – a coincidence of expression and meaning) impossible. He feels impelled to 'catch the drivel' of the bitch in question, and moreover to *ask* the ass about his 'fool research' (*CP*, 181). Yet he is caught in a frightening bind; in the final lines, he observes:

> Oh hell,
>
> Only the young can be alone freely.

In his private life, he experiences the hell of ageing and anxiety, and time becoming increasingly 'shorter now for company' (*CP*, 182). Crude language in this poem, then, is intended to reflect the desperation which the poet feels about this frustrating situation. It carries a note of urgency. As in other poems in *High Windows*, it seems the language of a man with his time becoming 'shorter now' continually, and suggests a kind of last ditch effort to say what he actually wants to say (*CP*, 182).

Larkin is always acutely sensitive to language, and in particular to the clichés which form the currency of most social discourse. He does not use foul language in 'Sympathy in White Major', but its very absence is significant. He reverses the effect of internal tension by the use of a long string of ridiculous, stock phrases which reflect an elaborate attempt to sound informal through bluff heartiness – and which miss the real point entirely. The attributes which the poet repeats in the poem, describe the perfect English gentleman in quaint, turn-of-the-century terms. He rehearses this for an audience of one – himself – in his 'private pledge':

> *A decent chap, a real good sort,*
> *Straight as a die, one of the best,*
> *A brick, a trump, a proper sport,*
> *Head and shoulders above the rest;*
> *How many lives would have been duller*
> *Had he not been here below?*
> *Here's to the whitest man I know –*
> Though white is not my favourite colour.
>
> (*CP*, 168)

His own assessment of this judgement undercuts the extravagant, hearty praise by not answering it in kind; in other words, the poet's response is correspondingly not filled with hyperbole or the proper kind of cliché. Part of what he covertly objects to in this poem is this kind of stilted language; and it is easy to see why he is drinking alone rather than in company.

When he chooses to use it in his poetry, coarse language can reflect a joyous kind of rebelliousness, and of somehow getting one's own back on the world, as in the pronouncement which ends 'A Study of Reading Habits': 'Get stewed: / Books are a load of crap.' (*CP*, 131). These lines become all the more amusing as it is unclear whether the advice is being offered to himself or to others. The phrase is also meant to undercut the clichés found in popular fiction; ironically, what Larkin actually satirises in this 'study' of reading is philistine taste in literature.

Coarse language also celebrates freedom from social conventions, as in the opening lines of 'The Card-Players':

> Jan van Hogspeuw staggers to the door
> And pisses at the dark. Outside, the rain
> Courses in cart-ruts down the deep mud lane.
> Inside, Dirk Dogstoerd pours himself some more,
> And holds a cinder to his clay with tongs,
> Belching out smoke. Old Prijck snores with the gale,
> His skull face firelit
>
> (*CP*, 177)

Pissing, snoring, belching, gobbing and farting are all of a piece with
the rain and wind outside and the card-playing, ale drinking,
opening mussels, and croaking 'scraps of songs ... about love' (*CP*,
177). This also fits in with the puns suggested by the names – Dirk
Dogstoerd, Jan van Hogspeuw, Old Prijck. Here, however,
everything 'bestial' is in harmony with the entire scene, and creates
a compelling vision of 'The secret, bestial peace!' (*CP*, 177). The
building surrounded by a storm is a rich and magical 'lamplit cave'
(*CP*, 177). The true glory of this scene is that the men are not
bothering about being polite to one another. They eat, drink, smoke,
sing and piss by themselves, as it suits them, in companionable
co-existence. It is a very different sort of party from that which the
poet envisions in '*Vers de Société*', and the eminent fitness of the crude
language reflects this. It rejoices and exults, providing the contented
'peace' which the poet in '*Vers de Société*' so notably lacks, either
alone or in company.

'Livings III' also celebrates the kind of male cameraderie and free
speech found in 'The Card-Players'. Here the college's high table is
liberated from the constraints imposed by a host, as they dine
'without the Master' (an occurrence which makes 'The port [go]
round so much the faster', which is all to the good) (*CP*, 188). The
dons indulge in wide-ranging conversation 'with no less ease':

> Which advowson looks the fairest,
> What the wood from Snape will fetch,
> Names for *pudendum mulieris*,
> Why is Judas like Jack Ketch?
>
> > (*CP*, 188)

The breadth of the discussion topics and the setting portrayed in the
poem suggest an earthiness and a virile, masculine bonding. The
scene is also enlivened by a slightly lascivious tone since, of course,
they are talking about women in discussing names for female sexual
parts. In addition, free speech is the hall-mark of this celebration;
the fact that 'oath-enforced assertions fly' shows how exhilarating it
is to make strong statements. The attraction of this kind of crude
language is that it occurs in a masculine context. In good environs
such as this one, it comes to the surface and is shared in a community
rather than being separated out, apart from polite, conventional
language, and used as an internalised comment which can never rise
to the surface and be spoken aloud.

Still another important aspect of this kind of diction is that of
Larkin's celebrated ability to speak to and for the common man,

which he does in blunt, Anglo-Saxon words. Yet at the same time, the effect seems carefully calculated. Larkin uses this kind of diction for its shock value, and he does this by undercutting sentimental or romantic scenes with bluntness. 'Sad Steps', for instance deliberately satirises the lyrical passages to follow by its first line, 'Groping back to bed after a piss' (CP, 169).

Sometimes, of course, the effect of crude language is purely that of stunning simplicity, as in the opening to 'This Be the Verse':

> They fuck you up, your mum and dad.
> They may not mean to, but they do.
> (CP, 180)

For bluntness, it would be hard to improve on these lines. In addition, there is the sophisticated use of something for shock value which also carries a literal meaning. Robert Crawford comments on the pun in these opening lines; the '[fucking] . . . up' here is intended to be literal as well as figurative.[66] In 'High Windows' the phrase also denotes a literal act:

> When I see a couple of kids
> And guess he's fucking her and she's
> Taking pills or wearing a diaphragm,
> I know this is paradise
>
> Everyone old has dreamed of all their lives –
> (CP, 165)

The phrase is used in this poem to convey a non-illusionary, 'less deceived', cynical stance taken up by the speaker, who calls something bluntly by its name. Still, the word 'fucking' has very different overtones from anything else; since it involves reference to women, it takes on a frightening, sinister quality. Belching, pissing or farting are masculine and virile activities: 'fucking' designates the sex act as dirty, repulsive – and sadistic: 'They fuck you up' (CP, 180). In 'High Windows', the poet uses this phrase in order to shock us with the force of his feelings of exclusion. The juxtaposition of words like 'fucking' (a recent invention of the younger generation) and 'paradise' (at once too precise and old-fashioned to be anything but an expression of the older generation, connected with a Yeatsian Byzantium) serves to emphasise the gulf that separates the generations.

Thus, in Larkin's continual striving for precision, coarse language is always used in his poetry for a specific purpose. It works for all the usual and expected reasons, in fact: to shock, to get attention, to express inarticulate fury. Such outrages as the poet sees can only be described and responded to in this fashion; in other words, in a language which is by common consent taboo – almost a non-language, something designed to create a *poem* with a hole in it. Finally, the point of this is that the crude language taps the inexpressible rage that the poet feels internally. It articulates – or begins to articulate – the things which politeness causes him to suppress. It says them indirectly, yet through a recognised code of language which at the same time tears a hole in language. Jim Dixon in Amis' *Lucky Jim*, locked in a similar position, fantasises about decorating the history department schedule with obscenities expressing what he actually feels about the merits of the staff and their courses. In a sense, profane language is what one *would* use if one revealed one's thoughts. This in part is why the poet in 'Sunny Prestatyn' responds so instinctively and strongly to the graffiti on the travel poster. Someone – the graffito writer who acts as spokesperson for the group – has said exactly what he thinks about the whole business.

Thus Larkin marshals a reservoir of 'unprintable' matter behind his poetry. It sometimes breaks through to the surface in a poem; it is always meant to disturb.

In one sense, Larkin is loud and boisterous in his complaints against minor irritations, since he cannot effectively complain against that which above all else consumes him: the imminent approach of death. Cursing what appears ludicrous becomes a way of cursing fate for simply having been born; something like Guy the Gorilla, whose fury was declared to be 'wordless but huge', Larkin's impassioned means of expression often seem vividly clear without being especially articulated. In this Larkin displays that art which conceals art. Philistines of any description are seldom poets.

6

Toads and Melancholy

'Philip Larkin feels that his image as a graveyard poet is a cliché, and
a misleading one at that', writes one interviewer, and though this
epithet does not entirely describe the tone of his work, Larkin's
poetry so repeatedly insists on the approach of death as to be
morbid.[1] His poetry often expresses a combination of wonder and
annoyance, as though he can hardly understand how existence could
be allowed to be so unbearable. This surprise at life's manifold trials
sets him apart from melancholy poets like Thomas Hardy and A. E.
Housman, who gently mock those who refuse to acknowledge and
accept the gloom which surrounds us. As the speaker in Housman's
'Oh is it the jar of nations' says, one may be anxious to set things to
rights from beyond the grave, but 'quarrelsome chaps in charnels /
Must bear it as best they can.'[2] Larkin's speakers *cannot* bear it, and
their sense of outrage expends itself in extravagant gestures and
against immediate objects. The 'graveyard poet' label is slightly
false, since Larkin's habitual melancholy is so clearly driven by
intense fury. The question is whether he is simply a complainer, a
'self-loather' and 'self-snubber', or, in Henri Coulette's apt phrase,
'Kid Sophocles'.[3] Death and ageing certainly occupy the foreground
in his work, making consciousness of them seem inescapable. The
expectation of death becomes a self-fulfilling prophecy about which
the poet can secretly congratulate himself; as 'Aubade' puts it
succinctly, 'Most things may never happen: this one will' (*CP*, 209).
He cannot be contradicted; and he seems to relish reminding us of
this truth.

   One effect of this insistence on death's approach is a tendency to
see life starkly. This creates a stimulating dialectic, because it is
constantly in motion, alternating from one view-point to the other.
C. P. Snow points out in another context the inherent instability in
this scheme: 'The number two is a very dangerous number: that is

why the dialectic is a dangerous process. Attempts to divide anything into two ought to be regarded with much suspicion.'⁴ Larkin capitalises on the energy to be derived from such a division. His poetry tends to veer back and forth between resignation and defiance – and this produces a continual juxtaposition of emotional extremes in many of his poems, particularly those which complain against limitations such as 'the toad *work*' (*CP*, 89).

'Toads' addresses the relationship between the burden of work itself and the 'something sufficiently toad-like' which lurks in the poet himself, both of which seem to work together to reduce him to passivity (*CP*, 89). Unable to assign blame definitely to either source, he remains hemmed in by both inner compulsion (a super-ego which restrains him) and by outer necessity (working is the only thing that pays the bills). The poem is a complaint against something which displeases the poet, but it does not attack the source of his difficulty. Although it begins by challenging the necessity of submitting to the immediate source of his annoyance ('Why should I let the toad *work* / Squat on my life?'), the poet never directly answers this question (*CP*, 89). Instead he launches into a series of comments about what *others* seem to do. He appears reluctant, in fact, to articulate the advantage of unseating the toad – so much so that he undercuts every attempt to urge himself to rebellion.

In spite of the strong case which he thinks can be made in favour of living on one's wits, the poet advances a number of reservations about the success of such a venture. Although 'lots of folk' seem to do it, this characterisation of them seems both vague and imprecise. Who does so and where, besides in the unspecified designation of 'Up lanes / With fires in a bucket' (*CP*, 89)? This seems the kind of generalisation that the poet might make if he had no clear conception of what living in such a situation would be like – or if he had no desire to find out. The poet cannot know exactly how these people feel about their lives, as the phrases at the end of successive stanzas hint, by their lack of strong conviction: 'They don't end as paupers'; 'They seem to like it'; 'No one actually *starves*' (*CP*, 89). Most important, though, the argument that 'if other people do it, why can't I?' in itself has no relevance to his own problem. He seems to invite digressions which distract him from the main issue.'

Another strategy which prevents him from rebelling against the constraints of the toad is the poet's insistence that his possible choices consist entirely of two extremes. One either continues to work and shouts '*Stuff your pension!*' or throws it all away (*CP*, 89). Since he allows for no middle ground, this forces him to remain where he is, because the only available alternative seems so stark. Further, there is no way out of the dilemma because inner and outer 'toads' balance each other equally. The last stanza posits:

> I don't say, one bodies the other
> One's spiritual truth;
> But I do say it's hard to lose either,
> When you have both.
>
> (*CP*, 89)

Through the course of this tortuous argument, what seems to be the answer to a simple question becomes a complex discussion of an insoluble dilemma. Like the hero in a Greek tragedy, the speaker can blame neither fate nor his own free will for his predicament and his inability to solve it; he only knows that it is not his fault.

'Toads Revisited' achieves the same sort of finely balanced tension between desire and necessity, which again does not so much consult the poet's own ambivalent feelings about work as it projects the problem onto other people. The reason he gives here for his distaste for *not* working is that it does not suit him to be one of the 'stupid or weak' who are 'dodging the toad' (*CP*, 147). The poet abhors the idea of becoming a marginalised member of society, painting this situation with vivid imagination. For the marginalised, he imagines 'Nowhere to go but indoors, / No friends but empty chairs' (*CP*, 147). The poem is problematic because the lives of these people are its most compelling and poignant aspect. He builds an entire argument against his own desertion of the toad work; yet it is based on their loneliness rather than his own inner conviction of what he desires.

Since complaints necessarily spring from some sense of grievance, the poet can easily sound like a whiner. Self-pity destroys the force of the poems – unless it is deflected into detachment, or travestied in a lugubrious groan of depression. Larkin usually manages to write it out in both ways, so that he can both complain authoritatively about undeserved hardship (the toad's hunkers are 'heavy as hard luck') and complain in a parody of egocentrism ('Yet it doesn't suit me') (*CP*, 89, 147). This kind of dialectic works well because death is the ultimate answer to both complaints; and Larkin never relaxes his sense of its overwhelming annihilation. This truth means everything and nothing. If every human effort is doomed to destruction and every person to non-being, then there is no point in adopting any but the most pessimistic, Hardyesque of stances. Yet, conversely, death can confer a sort of importance on the present, and result in a keen sense of invigorating *carpe diem*. The mere fact of death can make living itself a hyperbole; every disaster can create 'the worst day of my life' and each day can constitute 'another step down Cemetery Road'.[5]

Larkin's comic poems on the subject of frustration often capitalise on his sense of grievance. 'Poetry of Departures' creates the same kind of comparison as 'Toads' and 'Toads Revisited', contrasting a wild, romantic impulse with a conservative, cautious one. The poet imaginatively identifies with another figure who has *'chucked up everything / And just cleared off'*, and who thus achieves retrospective glory (*CP*, 85). The resulting dialectic turns between the poet wanting to be like the rebel and yet not wanting to be like him. He can be sympathetic to the man's desire for finality (*'He walked out on the whole crowd'*), while at the same time remaining prudent and sensible about the difficulties involved (it seems 'so artificial') (*CP*, 85). The important point is not the question of which course the poet will choose, as this is a foregone conclusion, but that his dissatisfaction is cast in terms of a stark set of choices. As the examples of the poet and the departed man illustrate, one either goes or stays. This provides an invigorating sense of tension, and dramatises every-day life enormously.

Larkin puts other characters – losels, louts, lecturers, clerks, the rebel who walks out – into the position of having to make choices. When he is seen to admire these characters, his admiration is always qualified in a way which deflates anything romantic or desirable about them. The rebel in 'Poetry of Departures', for instance, is graced by the admiration of the crowd left behind, and yet it is also ironically his 'epitaph' (*CP*, 85). Although the poet expresses envy for a man braver than he, he casts a deflating glance at the anti-hero as well. The rebel's gesture of renunciation appeals as an exercise of power; but the poet makes it seem, from one perspective, an empty, artificial one. Both men end by appearing slightly depleted and ridiculous, the one man stalking off to crouch in the forecastle, the other reading good books on the bed. Further, the poet parodies his own emotional excitement in contemplating the gesture, describing it in the clichés of popular fiction, in phrases such as: *'Then she undid her dress / Or Take that you bastard'* (*CP*, 85).

Many of Larkin's poems are exercises in thinking problems through; he does this either by imagining he is someone else or by comparing himself to someone else. By revealing the weaknesses in several successive choices, he seems to create an overwhelming number of obstacles to any reasoned decision. As he sets out these seemingly insoluble problems, he then rejects or criticises every possibility for change; and his circular, evasive arguments reflect the existence of this frustration. Thus, rather than taking the role of a rebel and throwing himself against or beyond limits, the poet bends his energy toward exposing the shallowness of possible escapes. Even if he were 'courageous enough' to follow the example of the anti-heroes, such a gesture would only be 'the stuff that dreams are made on' (CP, 89). By implication, dreams are dangerous to indulge in. Yet a tension results from this constant vigilance against giving way to wild and romantic impulses; although Larkin rigorously rejects fantasies, he nonetheless must ponder and describe them in the process of correcting his impulses toward them. It is an instance of having things both ways: protesting yet momentarily embracing objects of desire.

As in 'Poetry of Departures', the language of escape fiction also moves the poet in 'A Study of Reading Habits'. In these poems Larkin writes about the attractions of a literature which enables one to make an imaginary leap beyond limitations one encounters in the world – or in one's own nature. One enters a new world and becomes the all-powerful hero who always wins. The reading process creates a new person, as the reader imaginatively becomes the fictional character:

> When getting my nose in a book
> Cured most things short of school,
> It was worth ruining my eyes
> To know I could still keep cool,
> And deal out the old right hook
> To dirty dogs twice my size.
> (CP, 131)

In the end, the poem works to dispel the illusion of being heroic, since by identifying himself with characters in fiction the poet ultimately reveals himself as dreary. Yet the poem achieves its irony in a curious way; we do not see how the poet made the transition from seeing himself as a hero to regarding himself as a clown or second-rate character. It seems logical to assume that he must have become disillusioned when he began to compare life to art and found it did not match; he has more in common with 'the dude / Who lets the girl down' than he does with the hero. This lesser figure seems 'far too familiar' – in fact, so like him that he knows he must identify with it (CP, 131). Yet it remains difficult to pinpoint the exact means of the change, since when he was a youth he knew that life was harsh and escape through books only partial; reading could cure 'most things short of school' – a fairly large item (*CP*, 131). And though he pronounces the result worth the sacrifice, reading did ruin his eyes; he reappears in adolescence with 'inch-thick specs' (*CP*, 131). Thus reading symbolically ruins his vision of reality.

Why, then, do these characters appear 'familiar'? It may seem as though the poet grew older and wiser about himself, and more easily able to distinguish between the unreality of escape fiction and the reality of dreary, every-day life. He can now see – indeed, cannot avoid seeing – the cowardice in himself that *makes* him not a hero. But he intuitively sensed it before, which is why he had to be reassured so repeatedly that he could *still* 'keep cool, / And deal out the old right hook' (*CP*, 131). The poem satirises the poet in suggesting that his latter choice is worse than his first. Drunkenness is like popular fiction because it too offers escape from consciousness of self.

Larkin's poems often take the form of dramatic monologues, which seem intended to reveal the poet's thoughts and feelings because he is speaking out of his own strong convictions. Yet the seeming directness of Larkin's complaints is often hedged about with irony; he may be slanting the argument in a given poem by exaggerating some points, or by saying one thing while thinking another. Although this emphasis on his own experience can seem slightly self-indulgent, it is what gives strength to Larkin's work; and as he points out, it reflects the example of his literary mentor, Thomas Hardy. Yet his own experience and his own way of shaping or commenting on that experience are markedly different from Hardy's. When Larkin indulges in self-pity, he often parodies it, as in 'Self's the Man', where he claims with mock ingenuousness: 'Oh, no one can deny / That Arnold is less selfish than I' (*CP*, 117). The initial pause induced by the word 'Oh' adds a further touch of priggishness to the whining which follows. In effect, no one can carry this sort of thing off gracefully – such self-centered complaints tend to make those who indulge in them seem petty. However, much of what drives these poems is their comedy; it is black humour of a kind that is elaborately self-deprecating. Larkin achieves this in part through sheer verbal facility; these sparkling, bitter poems have something of the character of light verse, but they are also structured in a way which lends them stinging irony – and which gives them substance. When Larkin divides things into two opposing sides, he usually seems to be carefully weighing them against each other, measuring their relative merits, and working around to a logical conclusion. Given this pragmatic, empirical bent, what surprises one is his not, in most cases, having reached a definitive conclusion after all. The seeming certainty in tone is often belied by devious indirection in the underlying net of logic in Larkin's work.

His tactic of comparison also enriches many of the poems. In the poems which are not parodies, such as 'Mr Bleaney' and 'Dockery and Son', the speaker makes an argument for sameness between himself and his double which actually stresses the difference between them. He uses other characters to define his own identity by contrast, ostensibly to say what he is, but in reality as a diversion in order to shift attention toward others and away from himself. In the same way that the misfits in the 'toad' poems provide an alternative to work, the men in these poems provide an alternative example to the poet's choice for solitude. For what they represent, these figures pose a threat to the speaker, who regards their example with either envy or horror, and who judges his own worth by comparison with them. The tone of wonder and annoyance present in 'Self's the Man' or 'Toads' modulates in these poems into studied detachment, but they pursue the same end: to define precisely or evaluate the speaker's position, and to do so in light of his desires.

'Mr Bleaney' turns directly on a comparison, as the former lodger of a rented room becomes the speaker's double. The contrast between the two men is heavily stressed; they are two distinct figures who are none the less identified with each other because they are both measured by the 'one hired box' of the rented room (*CP*, 103). The differences between the men are quite clearly delineated: Mr Bleaney is an extrovert, who was favoured by the landlady and whose voice continues to chatter in the form of the 'jabbering set he egged her on to buy'. The poet is an introvert – his desire is for room for books, his action to lie on the bed, his only verbal comment a terse ' "I'll take it" ' (*CP*, 102). There is a flatness and prevailing gloom in this description; yet despite its stark divisions, the poet tries to come to grips with a larger question through an emphasis on uncertainty rather than on certainty. For all his transparency, the departed Mr Bleaney remains a mystery. It is impossible to know what he thought. This poem has the strange, lucid quality of a murder mystery or spy novel, where the investigator tries to reconstruct a dead or departed man's life and thoughts. The dialectic inherent in the poem keeps broadening out into certainty – Bleaney seems to have been such a simple fellow that we feel we have him taped – and then collapsing into uncertainty.

The poem constitutes a private argument, signalled by the word 'but' in the final, long sentence which takes up the last two stanzas; and it asks a complicated and involved question (*CP*, 102). Did Mr Bleaney feel 'measured' by his surroundings? The poet himself feels undervalued – or aghast that he measures so little in these terms. The premise holds that *if* Mr Bleaney saw himself measured in this light (i.e. – as inadequate and 'worth' almost nothing as reflected in his bare lodgings) the poet '[doesn't] know' (*CP*, 103). This understatement, achieved in the most oblique way, suggests uncertainty in an otherwise stark and obvious situation and serves to reinforce the pessimism inherent in the poem. Whether or not Mr Bleaney felt small, the poet does; and in part, of course, he is simply expressing his own feelings through the departed Mr Bleaney.

'Dockery and Son' also turns on the poet's comparison with a very similar figure, this time with a college contemporary. Again, as in 'Mr Bleaney', the poem reveals the process of resolving an emotional crisis, one which has all the more force because the comparison of himself to Dockery comes upon the poet unexpectedly, and subsequently takes several stanzas to work out. Part of what gives both poems their emotional force is the relatively vulnerable position in which the poet finds himself. 'Dockery and Son' catches him in a moment of involuntary emotional regression. Seeing one's former teachers, even when one is grown to adulthood, almost invariably reinstates the original relationship, and in his conversation with the Dean, the poet vividly imagines this to be so:

> Or remember how
> Black-gowned, unbreakfasted, and still half-tight
> We used to stand before that desk, to give
> 'Our version' of 'these incidents last night'?
>
> (*CP*, 152)

Memories can have peculiar power, which is perhaps why Larkin makes no attempt in any of his work to recall his childhood. A letter to Barbara Pym reveals his distrust of them and helplessness in their presence:

> Then, one *does* get depressed sometimes, has anyone ever done any work on why memories are always unhappy? I don't mean really unhappy, as of blacking factories, but sudden stabbing memories of especially absurd or painful moments that one is suffused and

excoriated by – I have about a dozen, some 30 years old, some a year or even less, and once *one* arrives, all the rest follow ... Why can't I recall the pleasure of hearing my novel accepted, passing my driving test – things such as these? Life doesn't work that way.[6]

The power of memory to grip one's consciousness is echoed in 'Dockery and Son', as the crisis of the present is underscored by the immediacy of the past. The poet must again assume his former position of having to explain away his guilt in the face of authority; his discussion with the Dean finds him still explaining his 'version' of 'incidents' in which he has been involved, as he is giving an account of his present life.

The compelling problem in the poem is that the poet cannot see himself, apart from the comparison he has begun to make between himself and Dockery – a comparison which causes him to divide possible choices into two opposing entities and to regard himself as having chosen the lesser part. Dockery has a son, while he has 'no son, no wife, / No house or land' (*CP*, 152). This division further penetrates to the question of intention – does one will one's destiny or not? 'Where do these / Innate assumptions come from? Not from what / We think truest, or most want to do' (*CP*, 153). The position defined by the poet is that one does not choose a course – one's 'innate assumptions' harden in retrospect into something which is and yet is not one's own intention (*CP*, 153). It 'leaves what something hidden from us chose' (*CP*, 153). This view stresses the action of a solemn, mysterious hidden agent; yet it insists on this with brutal force, leading on to the poem's final lines:

> Life is first boredom, then fear.
> Whether or not we use it, it goes,
> And leaves what something hidden from us chose,
> And age, and then the only end of age.
>
> (*CP*, 153)

This is startlingly flat, and since it is clearly not meant to be funny in the way that 'Give me your arm, old toad; / Help me down Cemetery Road' is, it is difficult to know what to make of it (*CP*, 148). 'Dockery and Son' seems not to be ironic, except in the sense that it proposes that one cannot effectively trace the cause of one's fortune or misfortune.

The poem constitutes an effort to understand a complex problem through addressing a precisely defined and seemingly simple situation; how did it come about that the poet has no son, and furthermore, that he never fully felt the lack until this moment in time? Despite his extensive musing on the subject, the poet tends to avoid directly answering this central point. The invocation of death as the great leveller does not answer the question of what he wants or of whether he truly misses what Dockery possesses. He tries to trace the source of his desires – something impossible to trace – by following cause and effect; it must have been what he wanted, since he did end up with it. But at the same time, he remains unsure about this, since he did not remember ever consciously choosing it. Even hindsight gives no clue, as it smudges things up into 'sand-clouds' (*CP*, 153). Thus cause and effect here are impossible to discern even when addressed in a rational way. The fact remains that Dockery has a son and the poet does not; Larkin sets certainty (the reality of choices) against uncertainty (the impossibility of knowing) in a problem which cannot be resolved even by the starkness of the closing lines.

The extraordinary vividness of the anger which drives many of Larkin's poems suggests not only energy but ingenuity; he seems able to keep his anger alive and vibrant for several decades, and to make it yield poetry. It rarely becomes thin or tired, as has much of the later work of the 'Angry Young Men'. This is not to say that anger is the aesthetic measure of Larkin's work, or that his poetry succeeds because it is able to bash his enemies, either real or imagined. Even so, I think his work is substantially deepened by his having been able to articulate this rage. It lends his poetry irony and prevents it being mere case studies of depression; though his poetry is often about depression, it does not depress the reader. As he wrote to Pym on first reading her moderately grim novel *Quartet in Autumn*, 'I seem to recall that some Greek explained how we can enjoy things that make us miserable'.[7] And he remains irrepressibly funny and irreverent towards his own most serious work; a parody which he wrote of 'Days' begins as follows: 'What is booze for? / Booze is what we drink. / They come, they shake us, / Time and time over. /Beer, whisky, schnapps and gin – / What can we drink but booze?'[8]

At the same time, much of Larkin's achievement is to have been so inventive in his poetry with such a stark subject as death. As Clive James has perceptively observed, 'It's an inherently less interesting proposition than its opposite, and a poet forced to devote his creative effort to embodying it has only a small amount of space to work in. Nor, within the space, is he free from the paradox that his poems will become part of life, not death. From that paradox, we gain.'[9]

In Larkin's poetry on the subject of mortality, there remains a group of poems which insist harshly on fear in the face of death, and which are both bleak and sinister. The most compelling example of this approach is 'The Old Fools', where the poet displaces his fear of death onto the aged. While on one level he seems to be shuddering at the horror of ageing itself, as its effects are seen in these people, his descriptions of them are too scathing to seem impersonal. One cannot help feeling that he hates the old fools themselves; and this is, naturally, the response he wants to catch us out in. 'We' shall not only 'find out'; we as readers are also implicated in his repulsion by finding that we share in it (*CP*, 197). The plight of the aged men and women – illness and dysfunction – is not their fault, yet in inverted logic the poet writes as though it were; at the least, he inquires why they do *not* protest, as he thinks would be only reasonable: 'Why aren't they screaming?' (*CP*, 196). This is hardly an equable view of the ageing process, nor does it seem intended to be so.

In other poems, his view of mortality is usually detached, and yet it is chilling and effective because of the very ordinariness and every-day settings he writes about. He stresses death's omnipresence; 'All streets in time are visited', proclaims 'Ambulances' (*CP*, 132). In addition, he continually highlights the modern technical, medical aspects of illness and mortality, dwelling on the 'frightening smell' which hangs in hospital corridors, the threat of rooms and 'rooms past those', and the inevitability of death (*CP*, 191–2). 'Aubade' proves that nothing can defeat or mitigate the horror and permanence of death. Yet death does not become a romantic figure in Larkin's work. Even in 'Cut Grass', the nature imagery is conventional and almost bland: 'Brief is the breath / Mown stalks exhale. / Long, long the death' (*CP*, 183). Death is never personified or romanticised; but this rescinds some of its power and provides the possibility of a cool and rational view-point.

This willed detachment also appears in 'Aubade', Larkin's most grim meditation on mortality – his 'in-a-funk-about-death poem', as he described it.[10] In 'Aubade' the poet tries to shrink death to ordinary proportions at the same time as confronting its inevitability. He does not diminish its power or immediacy; he adopts a dry, courteous tone with it. And this reasonableness exhibits another kind of stoicism – a kind that does not deny the panic of the deathbed, but which offers in 'Days' an understated poem about life and death. 'What are days for? / Days are where we live' (*CP*, 67). Their ceasing to be creates a frozen picture of completely meaningless activity, bringing 'the priest and the doctor

/ In their long coats / Running over the fields' (*CP*, 67). Scrupulously recording the inevitability of ageing and death, Larkin does not argue against death so much as against our illusions about it. In 'Next, Please' he insists that we put aside transitory, ill-founded hopes and see the 'black- / Sailed unfamiliar' approaching (*CP*, 52).

In many of these poems, Larkin seems to be attempting to face death without flinching by being conscious of its inexorable approach. On occasion, this gives his work a tone of morbid self-congratulation; it is an incontrovertibly accurate prophecy, and for Larkin personally it was a much-dreaded and deeply contemplated one. Larkin's father died of cancer at the age of 63; his friends have pointed out that Larkin dreaded a similar fate, and said for years that he himself would die at the same age as his father.[11] Like this episode from his life, there is something macabre in his poetry on the subject.

Larkin's vision is fundamentally different from that of Hardy and Housman because they see the grimness continuing after death. They write of corpses complaining of their rest being broken, and 'chaps in charnels' worrying about present-day gunfire and the war of nations, or inquiring about their sweethearts from the grave. But Larkin sees death as the great annihilator; no one, in his view, will be around to be either disillusioned or betrayed after death. As 'The Old Fools' describes it:

> At death, you break up: the bits that were you
> Start speeding away from each other for ever
> With no one to see.
>
> (*CP*, 196)

From beyond the grave, it is impossible even to look back on the 'sand-clouds' which rear behind, embodying one's choices. He does not expect his perspective to be understood; 'my secretary clearly thinks I'm mad', he wrote once in passing to Betjeman, on the subject of his obsession with mortality.[12] At the same time, the amazing thing is perhaps not Larkin's pessimism, which is very credible in its way, but his ability to see a glimmer of comedy despite it. His witty caution to a younger poet, Andrew Motion, on the occasion of his thirtieth birthday is a case in point: 'The 30s are super. The 40s even better. So don't worry. Yet.'[13] Larkin remained able to joke about ageing to the end, and to create a poignant contrast on his own account, writing to Douglas Dunn in his last illness: '[the] doctors assure me that I shall be a new man in a few months' time. Personally, I liked the old one, but he seems to have gone for ever.'[14] This view must also be set against the compelling final vision of Larkin in Andrew Motion's brilliant elegy for the poet, part of which describes Larkin's words on a last visit in hospital:

> *The trouble is, I've written*
> *scenes like this so many times*
> *there's nothing to surprise me.*
>
> *But that doesn't help one bit.*
> *It just appals me.*[15]

In living with and writing about this agonising tension between transient life and certain mortality, Larkin composed elegies which often sounded like satires, and inarticulate howls which were also carefully reasoned formal poems. His life's work seems – in its 'vivacious melancholy' – to exemplify the paradox of another poet, Henri Coulette, who once remarked upon the passing of a crisis during the illness which finally took his life: 'The good news is, I'm going to live. The bad news is – I'm going to live.'[16]

Notes

Introduction

1. Philip Oakes, 'The unsung old medallist: Portrait of a poet', *Sunday Times Magazine* (27 March 1966), p. 63.
2. Larkin to Pym, PYM MS 151/74, 18 July 1971. (All Pym manuscripts are lodged in the Bodleian Library.) Permission to quote from all unpublished material has been given by individual holders of manuscripts and by Larkin's literary executors.
3. *ibid.* fol. 57, 8 October 1969.
4. Philip Oakes, 'The unsung gold medalist', p. 65. Conversation with Douglas Dunn.
5. Alan Bennett, 'Diary', *London Review of Books* (18 December 1986), p. 21.
6. Letters to Douglas Dunn, MS DDD/8, 26 February 1972, 4 March 1984. Letters lodged in the Brynmor Jones Library, owned by Douglas Dunn.
7. A. Kingsley Weatherhead, *The British Dissonance: Essays on ten contemporary poets* (Columbia, Missouri: University of Missouri Press, 1983), pp. 3–4.
8. For a full discussion of this subject, see Chapter 1, 'Larkin and the Movement', in David Timms, *Philip Larkin* (Edinburgh: Oliver & Boyd, 1973).
9. Larkin to Douglas Dunn, MS DDD/8, 7 November 1975.
10. Larkin wrote to Pym on the occasion: 'Did I tell you I got my gold medal through the post? It turned up when I was shaving one morning. Alas, for my dreams of entering high society! "We are told that you are the best poet in our Empire, Mr Larkin" – fat chance.' Larkin to Pym, PYM MSS 151/42, 13 January 1967.
11. John Horder, 'Poet on the 8.15', *Guardian* (20 May 1968).
12. Larkin to Rossen, undated 1984[?]. Lodged in Brynmor Jones Library.
13. Larkin to Betjeman, 5 January 1966. Letters lodged in the University of Victoria Library.
14. Larkin to Pym, PYM MS 152/32, 21 August 1978.
15. Andrew Motion, *Philip Larkin* (London: Methuen, 1982) p. 28.
16. Larkin to Sutton, DP/174/2, July 1949. Letters lodged in Brynmor Jones Library.
17. Larkin to Rossen, 23 May 1985. The particular subject he referred to in this letter was a special session on Larkin's work at the Modern Language

Association Convention in 1985, chaired by Dale Salwak. Books on Larkin by Alan Brownjohn, Lolette Kuby, Bruce Martin, David Timms, Simon Petch, Terry Whalen and Andrew Motion attest to the interest which he holds for scholars. Recently published work includes a collection edited by Dale Salwak, *Philip Larkin: The man and his work* (London: Macmillan, 1989) and Larkin's *Collected Poems*, edited by Anthony Thwaite (London: Faber & Faber, 1988); the official biography is currently being written by Andrew Motion.

Chapter 1

1. Barbara Everett, 'Larkin's Edens', *English* (Spring, 1982) p. 41.
2. Barbara Everett, 'Larkin and us', review of Anthony Thwaite, (ed.), *Larkin at Sixty*, in *London Review of Books* vol. 4, (no. 20, 1982).
3. Conversation with Charles Monteith, 11 September 1987.
4. Larkin to Sutton, MS DP/174/2, 21 May 1941.
5. *ibid.* 24 September 1941.
6. *ibid.* 26 March 1941.
7. A. Alvarez has usually been cast as Larkin's main detractor, though others have been markedly sceptical of his work as well. (See A. Alvarez, 'Verse chronicle: Philip Larkin', *Beyond All this Fiddle* (London: Allen Lane, 1968).)
8. J. R. Watson, 'The other Larkin', *Critical Quarterly* vol. 17, no. 4 (1975) 347.
9. Among the most eloquent defenders of Larkin's reputation are John Wain, Clive James, Barbara Everett, Andrew Motion, and the contributors to Anthony Thwaite's edited volume of tribute, *Larkin at Sixty*, (London: Faber & Faber, 1982).
10. John Wain, 'The importance of Philip Larkin', *Oxford Magazine*, no. 7 (Fourth week Hilary Term, 1986). p. 8.
11. Grevel Lindop, 'Being different from yourself: Philip Larkin in the 1970s', Peter Jones and Michael Schmidt, (eds), *British Poetry since 1970: A critical survey*, (New York: Persea Books, Inc., 1980), p. 52.
12. John Press, *A Map of Modern English Verse* (London: Oxford University Press, 1979) p. 254.
13. Andrew Motion, *Philip Larkin* (London: Methuen, 1982), p. 26.
14. Alan Brownjohn, 'Novels into poems', Anthony Thwaite, (ed.) *Larkin at Sixty*, p. 109.
15. Larkin to Sutton, MS DP/174/2, 20 December 1940.
16. *ibid.*
17. *ibid.*
18. *ibid.* 13 July 1949.
19. *ibid.* 16 April 1941.
20. *ibid.* 7 May 1941.
21. *ibid.* 16 June 1941.
22. *ibid.* 13 July 1949.
23. *ibid.* 29 June 1942.
24. *ibid.* 20 December 1940.
25. *ibid.* 20 September 1945.
26. *ibid.* 11 April 1945.

27. *ibid.* 16 August 1946.
28. Larkin to Pym, PYM MS 151/ 21, 20 February 1964.
29. Larkin to Sutton, MS DP/174/2, 20 September 1945.
30. *ibid.* 28 April 1947.
31. *ibid.* 10 July 1947.
32. *ibid.* 28 October 1947.
33. *ibid.* 11 August 1948.
34. *ibid.* 28 July 1946.
35. *ibid.* 20 May 1950.
36. *ibid.* 6 October 1948.
37. *ibid.* 17 October 1945.
38. The following references to Larkin's working notebook refer to the manuscript which he donated to the British Museum. Larkin MS 52619, fol. 80.
39. *ibid.*
40. Larkin eventually made this poem the closing piece in *The Less Deceived*. It turns out that this is the third poem chronologically to have been composed for eventual inclusion in *The Less Deceived*, and actually to have been the first in the main bulk of the composition of this work. 'Going', which seems very similar in tone and imagery to the poems in *The North Ship*, was written in 1945, 'Wedding-Wind' in September of 1946. 'At Grass' first appears on 3 January 1950, some four years later, and heralds a continuous outpouring of poems from that point on, which eventually became collected in *The Less Deceived*. Ten poems were completed in 1950, three in 1951, four in 1953, and nine in 1954. Another significant aspect of this development is that Larkin himself was personally interested in these dates of composition: he compiled a list of poems and their dates of completion.
41. It was eventually published in 1954 in *Essays in Criticism* vol. 4, p. 86.
42. Larkin MS 52619, fol. 98.
43. *ibid.* fol. 90.
44. *ibid.* fol. 89.
45. *ibid.* fol. 90.
46. *ibid.* fol. 91.
47. *ibid.* fol. 90.
48. *ibid.*
49. *ibid.* fol. 91.
50. *ibid.*
51. Larkin continued to write during the period between 1948 and 1955, as the British Museum manuscript shows. Further, he seems to have felt so strongly about publishing his work that he arranged for a collection of poetry to be privately printed in 1951, in a pamphlet entitled XX *Poems*. These were in fact sent out to various people in hopes of attracting favourable notice, though they failed for the most part to evoke response. B. C. Bloomfield's bibliography notes the following mishap: 'Most of the copies were sent by the author to prominent literary figures who generally did not acknowledge receipt, insufficient stamps having been put on the envelopes because postage rates had just been raised' (B. C. Bloomfield, *Philip Larkin: A bibliography 1933–76* (London: Faber & Faber, 1979 p. 33).
52. Larkin to Sutton, MS DP/174/2, 1 April 1941.
53. Larkin, 'Reputations revisited', *Times Literary Supplement* no. 3,906 (21

January 1977), 66.

54. Larkin to Sutton, MS DP/174/2, 1 April 1941.
55. *ibid.* 28 January 1948.
56. *ibid.* 24 April 1951.
57. *ibid.* 24 April 1951.
58. *ibid.* 2 January 1951.
59. Larkin to Pym, PYM MS 151/ 88, 22 January 1975.
60. Larkin to Pym, PYM MS 151/ 88, 22 January 1975.
61. Larkin to John Betjeman, 17 June 1976.
62. Terry Whalen, *Philip Larkin and English Poetry* (London: Macmillan, 1986) p. 5.
63. Andrew Motion, *Philip Larkin*, p. 82.

Chapter 2

1. Timms lists several lines which Larkin borrowed virtually intact from Yeats. See David Timms, *Philip Larkin* (Edinburgh: Oliver & Boyd, 1973), pp. 26–7.
2. John Horder, 'Poet on the 8.15', *Guardian* (20 May 1965), p. 9.
3. Some critics have pointed out similarities between Larkin and Wordsworth: see John Bayley, 'Larkin and the Romantic tradition', *Critical Quarterly* vol. 26, nos 1 & 2 (1984) and Michael Tierce, 'Larkin's "Like the Train's Beat"', *American Notes and Queries* vol. 1, no. 1, (January 1988) pp. 21–3. Interestingly, John Betjeman saw Larkin in much the same light. He write to him on the publication of *High Windows* with commendation for capturing an essential England: 'It has that sense there always is with you that there is also with Wordsworth, namely that we are part of a revolving universe' (Letter from Betjeman to Larkin, 31 May 1974).
4. Timms notes the ambivalence in the poem's ending: 'The "almost-instinct" may be misguided, but it is valuable and affecting as an enduring feature of human relationships.' He goes on to characterise Larkin's stance here as 'unsentimental charity' (David Timms, *Philip Larkin* (Edinburgh: Oliver & Boyd, 1973), p. 109).
5. J. R. Watson, 'The other Larkin', *Critical Quarterly* vol. 17, no. 4, 1975, p. 354.
6. Anthony Thwaite, 'Philip Larkin', *Contemporary Poets*, J. R. Murphy (ed.), (London: St James Press, 1970), p. 629. Thwaite writes: 'some readers have mistakenly supposed that Christianity is ... being endorsed, which in fact is what the poem sets out with great pains *not* to do.' He adds, 'There is agnostic stoicism in [Larkin's] work, which confronts change, diminution, death with sardonic resignation.'
7. Conversation with Maeve M. Brennan, former Sub-Librarian, Brynmor Jones Library.
8. The illusory voice which calls in Larkin's 'Faith Healing' seems uncannily like the one in the last lines of George Herbert's 'The Collar': 'But as I rav'd and grew more fierce and wilde / At every word, / Me thoughts I heard one calling, *Child!* / And I reply'd, *My Lord.*' (George Herbert, *The*

Works of George Herbert, F. E. Hutchinson, (ed.), (Oxford: Clarendon Press, 1941) pp. 153–4.)

9. Motion sees the 'dialectic' between a Yeats and Hardy influence in Larkin's poems as constituting 'an expression, within the structure of Larkin's vocabulary, of his divided response to the world: it mirrors and vitalises a continual debate between hopeful romantic yearning and disillusioned pragmatism' (Andrew Motion, *Philip Larkin* (London: Methuen, 1982), p. 38). See also Terry Whelen, *Philip Larkin and English Poetry* (London: Macmillan, 1986), pp. 2–4.

Chapter 3

1. Poet and critic Donald Davie seems to have been the first to give Larkin this title, but several succeeding critics have used it as well.
2. Robert Crawford, 'Larkin's English', *Oxford Magazine* no. 23 (Fourth Week, Trinity Term, 1987), p. 4.
3. In part, Larkin was probably seen in connection with the post of Poet Laureate because Sir John Betjeman actually held the office at the time *The Whitsun Weddings* was published; the two men were friends, and admired each other's work.
4. Larkin to Pym, PYM MS 151/ 56, 18 March 1969.
5. *ibid.* fol. 45, 3 October 1967.
6. Dan Jacobson, 'Philip Larkin', *New Review* vol. 1, no. 3, (1974), p. 25.
7. Larkin to Pym, PYM MS 151/ 47, 1 July 1968.
8. David Timms, *Philip Larkin* (Edinburgh: Oliver & Boyd, 1973) p. 119.
9. This page from Larkin's working notebook was displayed in the Larkin Exhibition in the Brynmor Jones Library of the University of Hull, 2 June –12 July, 1986.
10. Larkin to Pym, PYM MS 151/ 58, 8 October 1969.
11. Andrew Motion, *Philip Larkin* (London: Methuen, 1982) p. 19.
12. Larkin to Pym, PYM MS 151/ 51, 11 November 1968.
13. *ibid.* fol. 72, 18 July 1971.
14. *ibid.* fol. 26, 7 December 1963.
15. *ibid.* PYM MS 152/ 33, 21 August 1978.
16. Larkin to Betjeman, 24 February 1976. The journey made such a strong impression on Larkin that a year later he was still remembering it. He wrote to Pym in 1977: 'how well I recall a year ago, and the dreadful journey to Hamburg! Thank Heaven we don't have to go through that again' (Larkin to Pym, PYM MS 152/ 4, 7 April 1977).
17. I am indebted to Professor and Mrs Rees for allowing me to quote this.
18. Larkin to Dunn, MS DDD/8, 2 July 1972.
19. Conversation with Andrew Motion and Anthony Thwaite.
20. Larkin to Pym, PYM MS 151/ 119, 28 November 1976.
21. *ibid.* PYM MS 152/ 51, 14 December 1979.
22. *ibid.* PYM MS 151/ 27, 7 December 1963.

Chapter 4

1. Larkin to Sutton, MS DP/174/2, 30 October 1951.
2. *ibid.* 20 November 1949.
3. *ibid.* 20 October 1941.
4. *ibid.* 15 September 1948.
5. *ibid.* 2 January 1951.
6. Drawing reproduced in description of Larkin letters to Sutton, *Christie's London* catalogue, Bouquet–3858, 22 June 1988, (London: Christie, Manson & Woods Ltd.), p. 51.
7. Larkin to Sutton, MS DP/174/2, 30 October 1951.
8. Jean Hartley, in BBC Radio programme 'The bicycle-clipped misanthropist', produced by Alistair Wilson (1986).
9. Terry Whalen, *Philip Larkin and English Poetry* (London: Macmillan, 1986) p. 43.
10. *ibid.* p. 44.
11. Kingsley Amis, *Lucky Jim* (London: Victor Gollancz Ltd., 1953), p. 39.
12. Andrew Motion, *Philip Larkin* (London: Methuen, 1982), pp. 57–8.
13. This line appears in the version of the poem published in *Critical Quarterly*, vol. 8, no. 2, 1966), and is altered in the *Collected Poems*.
14. Mayhew describes his aim in his preface to this massive study as follows, calling his book the 'first attempt to publish the history of a people, from the lips of the people themselves – giving a literal description of their labour, their earnings, their trials, and their sufferings, in their own "unvarnished" language'. He goes on to stress that he hopes not to sentimentalise the distress under which the poor suffer, but rather: 'My earnest hope is that the book may serve to give the rich a more intimate knowledge of the sufferings, and the frequent heroism under those sufferings, of the poor'. Henry Mayhew, *London Labour and the London Poor. A cyclopaedia of the condition and earnings of those that will work, those that cannot work and those that will not work: Volume I* (London: Griffin, Bohn & Co., 1861), pp. iii – iv.
15. David Timms, *Philip Larkin* (Edinburgh: Oliver & Boyd, 1973), p. 59.
16. Bruce Martin, *Philip Larkin* (Boston: Twayne, 1978), p. 48. Lolette Kuby also writes somewhat dismissively of the girl's misery, claiming that 'Her suffering excludes frustrated expectation and disillusionment. The man, on the other hand, the victimiser ruthlessly fulfilling his will, is nature's fool because it is not his will. His readings had become "erratic" (and erotic), a wandering from reason and humanity, a misreading' (Lolette Kuby, *Philip Larkin: An uncommon poet for the common man* (The Hague: Mouton, 1974), p. 47). Still, this reading of the man's misreading seems excessively abstract and distanced.

Chapter 5

1. Kingsley Amis, *Lucky Jim*, (London: Victor Gollancz Ltd., 1953) p. 53.
2. Larkin to Sutton, MS DP/174/2, 26 November 1944.
3. Barbara Everett, 'Art and Larkin', Dale Salwak (ed.) *Philip Larkin: The man and his work*, (London: Macmillan, 1989), p. 133.
4. This phrase appears in J. R. Watson, 'The other Larkin', *Critical Quarterly*, vol. 17, no. 4 (1975), p. 348.
5. Jean Hartley in BBC Radio programme 'The bicycle-clipped misanthropist', produced by Alistair Wilson (1986).
6. Larkin to Sutton, MS DP/174/2, 'Thursday', 1939 [?].
7. *ibid*. 26 June 1946.
8. Bruce Martin (among other critics) suggests a direct correspondence between them, though Amis categorically denies this except in small details. At the time Amis was writing the novel, Larkin lived in a street called Dixon Lane; furthermore, he was the novel's first reader – he read its early drafts. Martin rightly suggests as well that 'the character of Lucky Jim was at least partly self-inspired' by Amis himself. (Bruce Martin, *Philip Larkin* (Boston: Twayne, 1978), p. 17.)
9. Philip Oakes writes, 'It is the voice of Larkin which rings, rancorous and clear, in the diatribes against "filthy Mozart" in Kingsley Amis's novel *Lucky Jim*.' Philip Oakes, 'The unsung gold medallist: Portrait of a poet', *Sunday Times Magazine* (27 March 1966), p. 65.
10. Conversation with Andrew Motion.
11. Larkin to Sutton, MS DP/174/2, 21 December 1942.
12. Conversation with Philip Larkin, 8 November 1983. He also, of course, made this statement publicly on other occasions.
13. Larkin to Sutton, MS DP/174/2, 29 June 1942.
14. *ibid*. 6 December 1946.
15. Kingsley Amis, *Lucky Jim*, p. 51.
16. Barbara Everett, 'Art and Larkin', p. 131.
17. Letter to Douglas Dunn, MS DDD/8, 4 March 1984.
18. *ibid*.
19. Robert Crawford, 'Larkin's English', p. 4.
20. Dan Jacobson, 'Philip Larkin', *New Review* vol. 1, no. 3 (1974), p. 26.
21. Conversation with Philip Larkin, 8 November 1983.
22. John Horder, 'Poet on the 8.15', *Guardian* (20 May 1968), p. 9.
23. Letter to B. Mackereth, 5 November 1966 (included in the Larkin Exhibition in the Brynmor Jones Library of the University of Hull, 2 June –12 July, 1986).
24. B. Mackereth in 'The bicycle-clipped misanthropist'.
25. Letter to M. Judd, M. Brennan and B. Mackereth, 25 July 1959, (included in the Larkin Exhibition).
26. Larkin to Sutton, MS DP/174/2, 20 December 1940 [?].
27. Kingsley Amis, 'Oxford and After', Anthony Thwaite (ed.), *Larkin at Sixty*, (London: Faber & Faber, 1982), p. 25.
28. Larkin to Sutton, MS DP/174/2, 'Monday night' 1939 [?].
29. *ibid*. 'Friday night' 1939 [?].

30. *ibid.* 29 November 1946.
31. *ibid.* 1 April 1942.
32. *ibid.* 4 August 1939 [?].
33. *ibid.*
34. *ibid.*
35. Michael Bowen in 'The bicycle-clipped misanthropist'.
36. Kingsley Amis, Obituary for Larkin, *Observer* (8 December 1985) p. 22.
37. Larkin to Sutton, MS DP/174/2, 21 December 1942.
38. *ibid.* 1 April 1941.
39. *ibid.* 21 December 1942.
40. A comment made in a letter to Barbara Pym suggests an almost wistful desire for a more specific audience: 'Actually almost nobody reads my *Telegraph* articles: just occasionally I get a letter asking where to buy records, or something like that.' PYM MS 151/ 19, 27 October 1963.
41. E. J. Hobsbawm, 'The Jazz comeback', *New York Review of Books*, (Feb. 12, 1987).
42. Robert Pinsky, 'The opinionated poet', *The New York Times Book Review* (12 August 1984) p. 9. Pinsky stresses Larkin's limits as a critic (likening him to 'a bar bore or an academic dinosaur clumsily baiting junior faculty'), though he also adds that 'Within these limits, Mr. Larkin writes movingly and illuminatingly about such topics as his work as a librarian.'
43. Letter to Pym, PYM MS 152/ 18, 20 September 1977.
44. *ibid.* Pym MSS 151/ 78, 22 March 1972.
45. *ibid.* fol. 12, 15 July 1963.
46. Robert Crawford, 'Larkin's English', p. 4.
47. Kingsley Amis, Obituary for Larkin, *Observer* (8 December 1985) p. 22.
48. Grevel Lindop, 'Being different from yourself: Philip Larkin in the 1970s', Peter Jones and Michael Schmidt (eds.), *British Poetry Since 1970: A critical survey*, (New York: Persea Books, Inc., 1980), p. 46.
49. Letter to Pym, PYM MSS 151/ 42, 13 January 1967.
50. '"A great parade of single poems" – Philip Larkin ... discusses his "Oxford Book of 20th-Century English Verse" with Anthony Thwaite', *The Listener* (12 April 1973), p. 472.
51. *ibid.* p. 474.
52. *ibid.*
53. Letter to Pym, PYM MS 151/ 63, 9 May 1970.
54. *ibid.* fol. 81, 24 March 1973.
55. 'A great parade of single poems', p. 474.
56. Letter to Sutton, MS DP/174/2, 'Monday Night', 1939 [?].
57. 'A great parade of single poems', p. 473.
58. Letter to Pym, PYM MS 151/ 49, 1 November 1979.
59. *ibid.* fol. 48.
60. Philip Oakes, 'The unsung gold medallist', p. 63.
61. Letter to Pym, PYM MS 151/ 91, 17 April 1975.
62. Philip Oakes, 'The unsung gold medallist', p. 63.
63. Letter to Prof. Garnet Rees, 3 April 1979.
64. Kingsley Amis, *Lucky Jim*, p. 64.
65. *ibid.* p. 251.
66. Robert Crawford, 'Larkin's English', p. 4.

Chapter 6

1. Philip Oakes, 'The unsung gold medallist', *Sunday Times Magazine* (27 March 1966), p. 65.
2. A. E. Housman, 'Oh is it the jar of nations', Charles M. Coffin (ed.), *The Major Poets: English and American* (New York: Harcourt & Brace, 1954), p. 462.
3. Henri Coulette, 'The thought of *High Windows*', *Southern Review* (1974) p. 44.
4. C. P. Snow, *The Two Cultures and the Scientific Revolution* (Cambridge, Cambridge University Press, 1959), p. 9.
5. Betty Mackereth and Michael Bowen in BBC Radio programme 'The bicycle-clipped misanthropist', produced by Alistair Wilson (1986).
6. Letter to Pym, PYM MS 151/ 73, 18 July 1971.
7. *ibid.* fol. 114, 27 September 1976.
8. Postcard/Christmas card: undated mid–1970s to K. Hibbert, (included in the Larkin Exhibition in the Brynmor Jones Library of the University of Hull, 2 June–12 July 1986).
9. Clive James, *At the Pillars of Hercules* (London: Faber & Faber, 1979), p. 59.
10. Letter to Pym, PYM MS 152/ 23, 14 December 1977.
11. Maeve M. Brennan in 'The bicycle-clipped misanthropist'.
12. Letter to John Betjeman, 14 January 1978.
13. Letter to Andrew Motion, (included in Larkin Exhibition).
14. Letter to Douglas Dunn, MS DDD/8, 5 August 1985.
15. Andrew Motion, '"This is Your Subject Speaking:" In Memory of Philip Larkin' *Natural Causes* (London: Chatto & Windus, 1987), p. 56.
16. The phrase 'vivacious melancholy' is quoted in Philip Oakes, 'The unsung gold medallist', p. 65.

Index